William Thomas Stead

The Pope and the New Era

Letters from Vatican

William Thomas Stead

The Pope and the New Era
Letters from Vatican

ISBN/EAN: 9783744674935

Printed in Europe, USA, Canada, Australia, Japan

Cover: Foto ©Lupo / pixelio.de

More available books at **www.hansebooks.com**

THE POPE AND THE NEW ERA

THE POPE

AND

THE NEW ERA

BEING

LETTERS FROM THE VATICAN IN 1889

BY

WILLIAM T. STEAD

CASSELL & COMPANY, LIMITED
LONDON, PARIS, NEW YORK & MELBOURNE
1890

CONTENTS

THE POPE AND THE NEW ERA.

CHAPTER I.

STARTING POINT.

In the following pages I attempt to discuss one of the greatest of all problems with, perhaps, as slender an equipment of qualification for the task as ever was possessed by mortal man. By heredity, by education, and by the associations and habits of a life-time, I am cut off as by a mental and moral abyss from the Church of Rome. Reared as a child on "Fox's Book of Martyrs" —fascinated in my youth with the revolutionary enthusiasm that convulsed Europe in the year of my birth, I have spent my working life in editing Radical newspapers—an occupation which left me neither leisure nor inclination for the studies necessary to enable me to appreciate the history of the past, or to command that gift of tongues without which it is impossible to converse in the present. It may, indeed, be said that my only

qualification was such an utter absence of all semblance
of qualification as to render it impossible for me to fall
into the delusion of imagining that I knew enough about
anything to exempt me from the duty of listening
patiently and attentively to every one who could speak
with authority upon the questions at issue.

The key to all right understanding is true sympathy,
and, so far as it is impossible for any one to sympathise,
so far it is impossible for him to understand.   Hence
the almost insuperable difficulties that beset me on my
road to Rome.   Not even the constant and helpful presence of friends whom I loved and respected, but whose
religious convictions I could not share, could overcome
the keen antipathies naturally excited by the political
heresies and theological superstitions that seem to be
rampant in Rome.   When one's forefathers have died in
battle, and perished at the stake, in protest against a
system which, by the inexorable logic of the law of its
existence, would, if it ever again had the chance, drive you
into armed revolt, if it did not stifle you by irresistible
force, it is somewhat difficult to cultivate that sympathy
without which the wisest of men can never obtain an inside
view of the realities of the Church.   Nevertheless, it is the
condition of success, and—so far as I may have been able
to obtain any clear insight into the problem which I went
to Rome to study—it is due to the resolute endeavour
which I honestly made to overcome the prejudices of a
life-time, and to examine the facts in a spirit of that
charity which hopeth all things, and of a faith which

revolts against the notion that a Church which to two hundred millions of our fellow creatures is the sole fount of Christian teaching has been utterly disinherited of God.

Two hundred millions of human beings form too vast a segment of our race for any one who looks at the world as a whole to be indifferent to the institution which, however imperfectly, constitutes their outward and tangible link with the Infinite and Ideal. I have been assailed—sometimes pretty fiercely—for the interest which I have taken in the Pope. The Catholic Church, I am told, is retrograde, reactionary, persecuting, opposed to the scientific spirit, the deadly foe of liberty, and the worst enemy of spiritual religion. To all of which representations I reply: Well, if so, what then? Under its colours march two hundred millions of our brothers and sisters. What is to be our attitude in relation to them? Can we excommunicate from our sympathies so vast a human host, or only regard them as a field for Protestant or free-thinking propaganda? That propaganda, so far as it is religious, has not made much progress since the days of Loyola, nor does the mere labelling this myriad "To be converted hereafter" help us much either to the ending or the mending of the Catholic Church. Granted that the Roman division does not march in the van, is that any reason why we should not do what we can to encourage by our sympathy the more energetic spirits to quicken the pace? In the onward march of Humanity towards the Ideal we cannot afford to ignore even the laggards in the rear. It may be, of course, that the utmost that outsiders can do by sympathy and encouragement will only produce an infinitesimal effect upon the dense and somewhat inert mass of the Catholic world. That is not my opinion. But, however infinitesimal it may be, it will at least be greater than that which is produced by intolerant denunciation of the whole system. There is great truth in the homely adage that you can catch more flies by a spoonful of honey than by a hogshead of vinegar, and it would not be amiss if our vehement polemists were to read anew the familiar fable about the contest between the sun and the wind as to which could most easily rid the traveller of his cloak. When people are damning each other daily, they are not very likely to excite each other to emulation in good works. Why are so many Protestants cased as in triple brass against all the influences—good or bad— that emanate from Rome? Surely it is because of the intolerance of the system against which they protest. Can they not see that their own intolerance produces exactly the same effect on those against whom it is directed, and that if they wish to permeate Catholicism with the Modern Spirit, the representatives of the Modern Spirit should not uniformly approach the Church in the mood of an executioner eager to drag his victim to the gallows? Excommunication is the worst instrument of conversion, although, alas! excommunication is the favourite weapon of mankind—whether it is exercised with the accompaniment of bell, book and candle, or couched in the disdainful sneer of a philosopher, or thundered from the platform of Exeter Hall.

I am a Briton, and I think, of course, that it would be better for the world if the French could wake up to-morrow thoroughbred Scotchmen. But that being impossible, we do not spend our time abusing the French because they are not Scotchmen. Nor do we attempt to get the most good we can out of our neighbours across the Channel by continually admonishing them of their deplorable depravity in being Frenchmen. Such an attitude would be utterly fatal to any hope of infusing English ideas into the French mind. But is not this what the non-Catholic world is constantly doing to the two hundred millions who were born Catholics, and who, despite all our propaganda, will die Catholics? By all means, let the propagandists go on with their mission. Healthy competition is the life of the world. But as the most sanguine propagandist does not dream, in his wildest optimism, of converting more than two million Catholics, would it not be well to preserve to the remaining 198 millions somewhat of the same respectful sympathy and generous recognition of their good points that nations have long since learned to show towards each other? In this matter the Church has lagged sadly behind the World.

Whether it is owing to invincible ignorance, or to the natural prejudices of race and education, I have never felt anything but repugnance to the Roman theology. But as an Englishman, accustomed from early years to feel that I formed a unit—however insignificant—of a world-wide empire, based on the free consent of free men, I have long felt the keenest interest in the only other empire which can for a moment be compared to our own in the number of its subjects, the diversity of its dominion, and the influence which it exerts on the destinies of mankind. As a mere problem of administration, the Catholic Church offers endless topics of interest for the study of an Englishman. The Empire of the Confessional, like our own Empire of the Sea, is based upon the voluntary consent of those who are its subjects. Authority there is in both systems—authority that with us speaks now and then through the loud-throated cannon, and at Rome by the spiritual artillery of the Vatican. But the real cement of both systems is the conviction of those belonging to them, that on the whole it is better to be within than without the fold. In one respect they differ. Our dominion is but of yesterday. Elizabeth and Cromwell were the earliest founders of the British Empire. The dominion of Rome was more than a thousand years old before the first Tudor sat on the English throne; its churches had encircled the world before our first colonists laid the foundations of Greater Britain. We are still in our lusty prime. But we are of mushroom growth, and the place which now knows us may know us no more, when the majestic fabric of the Catholic Church may still tower above the world as imposing as it was in the days when Charlemagne was crowned in the Church of St. Peter,

as majestic as when Leo drove Alaric from the city of
the Holy See. That, however, is not its chief interest.
Those who have to deal with the real and living forces
of the world cannot ignore the influence for good or for
evil which the Church commands. Like a mighty river
which drains a continent, it cannot be destroyed. It
may be drying up—but if so, the process is so slow
as to be almost imperceptible. It may have over-
flowed its banks, filling the lowlands with marsh, where
miasma breeds ague and fever, but it is there—and
cannot be got rid of. Huge mud banks may have
choked its channel, rendering it unnavigable; snags
may abound; the whole stream, whether as motive force
or irrigating source or inland waterway, may have become
utterly waste; but so long as it exists it must be reckoned
with, and, if possible, utilised. Opinions may differ as
to how far it can be utilised, but something more can
surely be made of it, from a purely secular point of view,
than we are making of it to-day. Such, at least, has
long been my hope—a hope which is deepening into a
conviction. This is not a dream of yesterday with me.
Years ago I wrote the following passage, which I quote,
in order to enable those who read these pages exactly to
understand the standpoint from which I approach the
subject:—

"A new Catholicity has dawned upon the world. All
religions are now recognised as essentially Divine.
They represent the different angles at which Man looks
at God. All have something to teach us how to make

the common man more like God. Questions of origin,
polemics as to evidences, erudite dissertations concerning formulæ, are disappearing, because religions are no
longer judged by their supposed accordance with Divine
Revelation, but by their ability to minister to the wants
and fulfil the aspirations of man. The individual, what
can it make of him? As it raises or debases, purifies
or corrupts, fills with happiness or torments with fear, so
it is judged to accord with the Divine will. The
credentials of the Divine origin of every religion are to
be found in the hearts and lives of those who believe it.
The old intolerance has disappeared, and the old indifference which succeeded it has well-nigh disappeared
also. The new tolerance of faith recognises as Divine
all the creeds which have enabled men to overcome
their bestial appetites with visions of things Spiritual
and Eternal.

"Nothing is more remarkable of late years than the
altered attitude both of Protestants and of Agnostics to
the great organization which has its seat, its centre, and
its capital in the Eternal City. The Catholic Church
towers above all secular organizations, much as the
majestic peak of the Matterhorn soars above the lesser
Alps which cluster round its base. Alike in antiquity,
in extent, and in the compact perfection of its fabric, all
other systems are but as the gaudy palaces of Cairo to
the Pyramids. This immense moral force, with its
princes in every capital and its priests in every village,
is no longer regarded as an enemy to be crushed so

much as an ally whose assistance cannot with safety be
dispensed with in the great task of ameliorating the
condition of mankind. Neither its evil traditions, nor its
intolerant dogmas, nor its extreme sacerdotalism, can
be allowed to blind us to the fact that it exists, and will
exist, as one of the most potent factors in the evolution
of morality and civilisation. What we have to do is not
to waste force in attacks which only accentuate its worst
features, but to welcome it into the broad arena of
humanitarian usefulness, and, weaning it from the
bigoted intolerance of the past, to summon it to renew
the triumphs of the early centuries in rebuilding the
City of God in the midst of an anarchic and distracted
world. The present Pope is a statesman of the first
rank, a philanthropist worthy the name, before whose
eyes flit fair visions of possibilities which may yet be
realised if he will live up to his privileges and rise to the
height of his unequalled opportunities. If, instead of
lamenting the dear dead past which returns no more,
and labouring to recall the for-ever-vanished temporal
sovereignty of the Italian Pontiff Prince over a second-
rate European capital, he were to turn his gaze to the
new dominion whose sceptre lies within his grasp, who
knows what might not be achieved? An Empire
dependent upon no trivial accidents of temporal
dominion, but one which the august representative of
the one universal, cosmopolitan organisation directed to
the attainment of moral ends might wield with universal
assent, is at his feet. He has but to will it in order to

step into the vacant throne, and to be accepted as the
natural leader of mankind in all good works. But however wistfully he may gaze at the prospect, his will be
but a Pisgah view. The Occidentalising of the Church
will not be accomplished till an Englishman or an
American sits in the Chair of St. Peter. In the mean-
time we must wait, encouraging, so far as is possible to
those who are without, any diversion of the immense
energies and exhaustless resources of the Church from
the barren polemics of the Middle Ages, and from the
mere propaganda of shibboleth and ritual to the fruitful
works of righteousness, of philanthropy, and of peace.

"Ours is the wider Catholicism, which accepts as the
Catholic truth only that which *quod semper, quod ubique,
et ab omnibus* has been held by mankind. It is tolerant
of all men, especially of the intolerant, who are always
in a majority. No differences of creed, of ritual, or of
label can blind us to the essential unity of the faith
of the Church Universal. That is of God which leads
men to act as God acted when He revealed Himself on
earth in the person of Jesus of Nazareth—even although
those who so act put the wrong label upon the Infinite
or ignore His existence. Handsome is that handsome
does. Christian is that Christian does. The man who
acts as Christ would do under the same circumstances
is the true believer, though all his dogmas be heretical
and his mind is in a state of blank agnosticism. The
true religion is that which makes most men most like
Christ. And what is the ideal which Christ translated

into a realised life? For practical purposes this: To take trouble to do good to others. A simple formula, but the rudimentary and essential truth of the whole Christian religion. To take trouble is to sacrifice time. All time is a portion of life. To lay down one's life for the brethren—which is sometimes literally the duty of the citizen who is called to die for his fellows—is the constant and daily duty demanded by all the thousand-and-one practical sacrifices which duty and affection call upon us to make for men. Hence the supreme Antichrist is selfishness, and he is farthest from his Divine Exemplar who converts even the ministrations of religion into the consecration of selfishness, which overleaps even the limits of time, and obtrudes its hateful egotism into eternity."*

It was not until 1889 that I had an opportunity of inquiring at first hand at the headquarters of the Catholic Church how far these aspirations were shared by the Holy See. A visit to Rome had been arranged in 1887, but the introduction of the Coercion Bill detained me in London. The opportunity did not recur till this autumn (1889). I left London in October, and spent three weeks in Rome. Thanks to the kindness of Cardinal Manning, I was received everywhere with the utmost cordiality. Not even in St. Petersburg were the authorities more courteous and, it seemed to me, more frank.

---

* This I wrote in 1887. It was published a year later in the *Universal Review*, December, 1888.

B

The prolonged discussions which I enjoyed with the Ministers of the Pope were, of course, confidential, but the net impression which they left on my mind is faithfully embodied in the following pages.

More of the letters from the Vatican have already been published. They appeared simultaneously in the *Pall Mall Gazette*, in more than a dozen of the leading papers in England, Ireland, Wales, Scotland, the United States, and Australia.* No such widespread publicity has ever before been commanded by any journalistic correspondence from Rome, a fact which is in itself of much greater significance than anything in the letters themselves. I have also embodied in this volume the greater part of an article which appeared in the *Contemporary Review* of July, 1889, entitled "The Papacy: A Revelation and a Prophecy."

I am well aware of the many defects in form and in substance of these letters from the Vatican.

---

* The following is a list of the newspapers in which the "Letters from the Vatican" appeared :—1, *Pall Mall Gazette*, London ; 2, *Freeman's Journal*, Dublin ; 3, *Birmingham Gazette* ; 4, *Liverpool Daily Post* ; 5, *Yorkshire Post*, Leeds; 6, *Northern Echo*, Darlington ; 7, *South Wales Daily News*, Cardiff; 8, *Western Daily Mercury*, Plymouth ; 9, *Dundee Advertiser* ; 10. *Glasgow Daily Mail* ; 11, *Cape Argus*, Cape Town ; 12, *Melbourne Argus*, Victoria. I have not yet received a complete list of the American journals which published the Letters, and I only know that the Syndicate agent informed me that they would have a still more extensive circulation were it not that many of the newspapers feared that the correspondence might offend their Catholic readers, "who are very numerous in the States."

There is much in them, I fear, which will give pain, and perhaps offence to those within and to those without the Catholic Church. That, however, was inevitable from the standpoint which I occupy. I would gladly have relinquished the task to any one who would have brought to it better qualifications than any which I possess; but those who are outside the Church did not think the Pope worth while troubling about, while those within are too much trammelled by their belief in the divinity of the institution to subject it unceremoniously to the investigation which, however imperfectly, I have honestly attempted to carry out. Therefore, as there was no one else who would do the work which seemed to me to want doing, I went myself. This little volume is the result.

CHAPTER II.

THE THREEFOLD QUESTION.

THE following was the first of the "Letters from the Vatican." It appeared in the last week in October :—

By far the most interesting question before the modern world is that which I have come to Rome to study within the walls of the Vatican. Everywhere the old order is changing and giving place unto the new. The human race is now at one of the crucial periods in its history when the fountains of the great deep are broken up, and the flood of change submerges all the old-established institutions and conventions in the midst of which preceding generations have lived and died. It passed through a similar crisis when the Roman Empire went down beneath the trampling feet of the Northern tribes. From the midst of that bloody chaos the Catholic Church evoked the imperfect Cosmos of modern Europe, which is now once more on the eve of transformation and supersession. To quote the testimony of an uncompromising Rationalist, it was the Papacy, a "spiritual despotism, which alone could control and temper the turbulent elements of mediæval society, could impose a

moral yoke on the most ferocious tyrants, could abolish
slavery, and infuse such a measure of pure and spiritual
truth into Christendom, as could prepare men for the
better phase which is to follow." What I have come to
Rome to try to discover, so far as may be possible, by
personal communication with the men who are now
charged with the guidance and direction of the Catholic
Church, is whether the agency which fashioned the Old
World that is now passing away is capable of even
attempting to play the same great rôle in the organisation and direction of the forces of the New Era, on
whose threshold we are standing to-day.

What are the distinctive characteristics of the new
era? They are three:—(1) The world is passing into
the hands of the English-speaking peoples ; (2) Society
is being reorganised on a Socialist basis; and (3) Woman
is at last beginning to be recognised as a being with
a right to equal privileges and opportunities with
man. When these changes are fully accomplished,
although there may not be a new heaven and a
new earth, yet all things will have become new. Taken
together, they amount to the most sweeping revolution
ever achieved on this planet. In their achievement
the human race will have to face many perils, to risk
the loss of much that it has acquired by the toils and
sacrifices of centuries, and to encounter risks—moral,
social, and political—at which the boldest may well stand
aghast. But Humanity turns not back. The timid may
cry halt, and the faithless may seek refuge in reaction—

" Yet not the less for them, we know,
    The eternal step of Progress beats
  To that great Anthem, calm and slow,
    Which God repeats."

Nothing that can be devised can prevent the consummation of this threefold Revolution.   It may be retarded, it may be guided, or it may be left to work itself out blindly.   What will be the attitude of the Catholic Church in relation to the immense problems now confronting the modern world?   Will it again essay to be the instrument in the hand of God for re-shaping the destinies of our race, or are its rulers so immersed in archaïc controversies as to be unable even to see the transformation that is going on around them?   It is one of the most momentous questions of our day.   For it amounts to an inquiry whether or not the Holy See can be relied upon as an effective moral force in the solution of the social, economical, and political problems that must be settled in one way or other by us and by our children.   Can we or can we not count upon the Pope and his Church for helpful human service in the coming times of stress and struggle through which we must pass in our way towards the New Order?

There are many to whom it will seem almost blasphemy to ask the question.   Some will resent it because they are so certain that the Pope is God's Vicegerent; others because they are not less certain that he is Antichrist.   Both are irrational.   The more Divine the Pope's mission, the better it will bear looking into ; and if he be

Antichrist, a closer examination will only make the truth the better known. My own stand-point is clear and simple. Seeing very clearly the immense perils that attend the evolution through which we are passing, it seems to me obvious that we should eagerly welcome every agency which may be, to any appreciable extent, a factor for good. There are not too many moral forces in the world for us to be able to afford to boycott any one of them. The Catholic Church is the only existing institution which faced a similar crisis to that through which we are passing. At that time, her bitterest enemies being judges, she did yeoman's service. She saved civilisation and humanised Europe. Possibly she may not be able to repeat the service. Her rôle may be exhausted. Her rulers may no longer be inspired. Here in the Vatican there may neither be an eye to discern the signs of the times, an ear to hear what the Spirit says to the peoples, nor a heart to dare to risk all for the salvation of men. That is what I have journeyed hither to discover; and for my part I can say, that no prejudice of early training or of religious conviction will for a moment stand in the way of my eagerly welcoming every indication of capacity and will on the part of the rulers of the Church to play their brave old rôle in the re-making of the world. Mankind stands too much in need of helpers in this crisis for any one to forget the wise old proverb which tells us that it is not wise to look a gift horse in the mouth.

Mazzini, who no doubt expressed the convictions of

most of those outside the pale of the Church, declared
fifty years ago that the Papacy was a corpse beyond
all power of being galvanised into life. Never again
could it be what once it was, the ruler and the director
of the conscience of the people. It had lost all moral
basis, aim, sanction, and source of action, and it had
become a lie and a source of immorality, because it
sought to perpetuate its authority after its mission was
fulfilled. Therefore, he argued, it was the duty of all
those who had at heart to win the City of the Future,
and the triumph of Truth, to make war upon the Papacy.
That was written half a century since, and the Papacy,
instead of descending into the grave which he declared
it had dug for itself, is much the liveliest corpse extant
to-day. During the nineteenth century, said Macaulay,
before it had run half its course, "This fallen Church
had been gradually rising from her depressed state and
reconquering her old dominion." That is even more
true to-day than it was when Macaulay reviewed Ranke's
"History of the Popes." It is still a great power. Its
voice is heard in every land. It has a garrison in every
parish. If it is not to be a blessing, it may be an infinite
curse. It is about time we ascertained which it is to be,
and what part it will take in the great Revolution.

Whatever we may think of the shortcomings of the
Catholic Church, it is still the only means of grace to
millions of human beings, who but for its ministrations
would grow up utterly ignorant of Christ and His
Gospel. Through its great mains and service pipes the

Water of Life is laid on into vast regions crowded with teeming millions, who would but for its agency have perished of thirst. However faulty it may be, it is a divine instrument for the salvation of men; and although we may wish it other than it is, if only for the greater success of its own mission, the Scarlet Woman conception of the Church may be profitably abandoned once for all. Burke, whose words of wisdom are always worthy of attention, gave it as his "humble and decided opinion" that "the Roman Catholic religion should be upheld in high respect and veneration, and that it ought tô be cherished as a good (though not as the most preferable good, if a choice was now to be made), and not tolerated as an inevitable evil." That, surely, is a more reasonable view of the great institution to whose head-quarters I have come to endeavour to gain some authentic information, if possible, as to the part which the Church will take in the great questions of the near future.

The first is the English peopling of the world. This is the most conspicuous political phenomenon of our day. It was the supreme merit of the Catholic Church that, amid the crash of the earlier world, it recognised with a sure prevision that the past was gone irrevocably, and that the future lay with the fierce warriors from the fastnesses and forests of the North. It remains to be seen whether the Church will be as quick to discern the salient feature of the great transformation through which the world is passing to-day. It is a revolution vaster and more rapid than that which founded the modern European world on the wreck and ruin of the Roman Empire. Europe is Byzantium. As the Roman Empire maintained a lingering death for a thousand years in the East, so the old world will continue to exist for some centuries. There will be wars and revolutions, and all the inane contests which are the modern counterpart of the feuds between the Blues and Greens in the Circus at Constantinople, but the centre of power will no longer lie in Europe. The new race that will dominate this planet will speak English. English laws, English customs, English literature, and, above all, the English habits of self-government and detestation of the militarism which is the blight of Europe, will be everywhere predominant. If the population of English speakers increases and multiplies at its present rate for another hundred years, there will be more people speaking English on the globe in 1989 than those who speak all the other European languages put together. Mr. Gladstone published some months ago a calculation that in the year 2000 the United States alone would contain a population of at least five hundred millions. An American statician calculates that the population of the British colonies will then have reached the figure of 176,000,000. Similar calculations show that the total population of Europe is not likely to exceed 534,000,000. If the increase of the English race were calculated at the ratio of expansion that prevailed from 1870-1880, it would in 1980 number 1,343,000,000. The world is passing into the hands of the English-speaking races. Already the English tongue is becoming the *lingua franca* of the planet. Already the territories over which the laws are made and justice is administered in the language of Shakespeare and of Bacon exceed in wealth, in extent, in the number of their populations, and in the limitless latent possibilities of their development, all other lands ruled by all other nations of the earth. In a hundred years, unless the progress of this marvellous transformation is suddenly checked in some manner as yet inconceivable, Italian, Spanish, and French will be but local dialects of as little importance, except for literature, as Erse and Welsh. Alone among the races the English have escaped the curse of universal military service. Alone among the nations they have learned to combine liberty and law, and to preserve an empire by a timely concession of local self-government. Whether we welcome or whether we deplore the prospect, the fact is unmistakable—the future of the world is English.

What, then, is to be the attitude of the Holy See in face of this strange re-making of the world? Upon the answer to that question depends the future of the Church. If she still aspires to exercise her beneficent dominion over the new and the coming world, she will follow the example of the great Popes who created Europe out of the chaos of barbarian invasion. She will no more seek to restore Papal sovereignty in the capital of Italy, than a thousand years ago she sought to revive the proconsuls of the Empire or to restore the

Cæsars.   Let the dead past bury its dead.   Rome, once
the world's centre, is now a mere provincial town, in an
out-of-the-way corner of a small inland sea.   The headquarters of the Church, in the days when she was a
living reality, gravitated by a natural law to the centre
of Empire.   If she is still to be a living reality, presiding
over the development of our civilisation and mothering
the children of men, then she will be true to the law of
her being, and establish the seat of her sovereign Pontiff
in the centre where sovereignty resides.   Rome is of the
old world, archaic, moribund, and passing away.   The
centre, the capital, and the mother city of the new world,
which Catholicism must conquer or perish, is not to be
found on the banks of the Tiber, but on the Thames.

Nor is it only on political, geographical, and ethnolo-
gical grounds that the Papacy must be Occidentalised—
Anglicised or Americanised.   The more sedulously the
Pope endeavours to fulfil his high mission, the more
necessary is it that he should avail himself of those plain
and simple principles of common-sense, applied to the
art of government, which are the pre-eminent endow-
ment of the English-speaking world.   These principles
are those of liberty and local self-government.   They
will never get a fair chance of being worked into the
bones and marrow of the Catholic Church until we have
a Pope who thinks English.

Secondly, the world is becoming Socialist.   Everywhere power is passing into the hand of the workman,
who is increasingly determined to use it so as to improve

the lot of the labourer. He demands to be allowed to live a human life. He protests against hours of toil being lengthened until he has no leisure left for his family or for himself. He demands to be allowed a just share in the wealth his labour assists to create. He is at war against a social system which cannot provide against periodical crises of depression and starvation, which houses him in hovels in which no horses would be stabled, and which dooms him in old age to the Bastille of the Workhouse. No doubt in this new quest for Justice much injustice will be done and more will be attempted, when the brute despair of trampled centuries

" Gropes for its right with horny, callous hands,
And stares around for God with bloodshot eyes ; "

and there is certain to be a good deal of ugly work done when brutes with the memories and desires of men

" Set wrong to balance wrong,
And physic woe with woe."

Hence the enormous importance of enlisting all the moral and intelligent agencies, whether in the Catholic or any other camp, in the work of guiding, educating, and directing these vast inarticulate forces, which tend more and more to dominate the future. What attitude will the Church adopt? On this point there are hopeful signs. The action of the Pope in reviving the crusade against the slave trade, which had almost become extinct, was a service to humanity worthy of the best days of the Mediæval Church. And the action of

Cardinal Manning in the recent strike of the dock labourers in the East of London has attracted the admiration of the world. The other day I received two newspapers—one from the Cape, the other from Constantinople. Both were full of eulogies of the great Cardinal. The *Turquie* concluded its leader by remarking that the struggle between labour and capital corresponded to the ancient war between civilisation and barbarism. The Church alone, it said, possessed the standing, the prestige, and the resources to enable it to play once more the mediator between the forces whose clash endangered Christendom. Is the Church as a whole going to act everywhere and always as Cardinal Manning acted in the dock strike? That is the question of questions at this hour.

Lastly, there is the great coming question, which contains in it more than any other issues vital to the progress of our race. Woman is beginning to acquire the status of a human being. In three-fourths of the world she is still a chattel of man. Nowhere is she a full citizen. But in England and in America she is beginning to arrive. The Anglicising of the world is a political problem. The Socialist movement is economical, but this last evolution is essentially moral. For weal or for woe, it will modify many accepted moralities. What has the Church to say to it—the Church which takes women and morals under its special care? Has it purged itself of the evil tradition of early times, which regarded woman as the handmaid of Satan, and carried the worship of celibacy so far as to seem to cast a slur upon the sacrament of marriage?

Such is a rough preliminary sketch of the questions for which I am seeking authoritative answers. If I fail, it will not be for want of patient, persistent interrogation of all those who are in a position to speak with authority at the Vatican. Before beginning the inquiry, my mind instinctively goes back to one of the most familiar of the stories of the Conquest of Canaan. When the host of Israel had just crossed the Jordan and were standing before Jericho, Joshua lifted up his eyes and looked, and behold, there stood a man over against him with his sword drawn in his hand. Instantly the Hebrew leader challenged the Unknown. "Art thou for us or for our adversaries?" It is a similar inquiry that I would address to the Holy See. And Protestant though I am by birth, education, and conviction, no one would rejoice more than I if on my ears should fall the welcome response, "Nay; but as Captain of the host of the Lord am I now come!"

CHAPTER III.

THE ANSWERS OF OUTSIDERS.

My opening letter not unnaturally excited considerable controversy. I received many letters and remonstrances. An English Nonconformist wrote to me:—

"I am, of course, at one with you in your appreciation of the service which the Roman Church has rendered and is rendering to the race. I also fervently desire that that Church may be made more helpful in this time of transition.

"But I cannot help perceiving that what you wish to hope from the Roman Church is for her to abandon her distinctive existence; her ecclesiastical *raison d'être*, and to turn her back on that history of her which, according to her distinctive theory, is a progress at heart infallible.

"Take your three points:

"(1.) The world is becoming English, and passing under English habits of self-government. That is to say, the world is becoming democratic. But the theory on which the Church is based is precisely the contrary to the democratic principle (which is Protestantism in politics). Romanism is essentially Cæsarism in religion. Peter, the Primate of the Apostolate and Vicar of Christ, along with his Papal successors, are spiritual, and, according to the idea of the Roman Church, are meant to be political autocrats. The world is becoming English and democratic, very largely because the English most emphatically asserted the autonomy of the individual. To ask the Roman Church to become English is to ask her to leap at a bound, so to speak, from the political state of Rome

in the second century to the political state of the American Republic
of the nineteenth century : to work at one spring the tract of progress covered by the slow development of Protestantism and
Puritanism during three centuries.

"But within the wider theory of the Roman Church is the narrow *practice* of Ultramontanism. All Catholic Europe outside
Italy groans inwardly over the persistent Italianism of the Papal
See. The Pope has (as a matter of history, generation after generation) seen Europe through Italian spectacles, and sacrificed the
German, the Gallican, the Anglican Church to his localism. Yet
you propose to His Holiness that at one gulp he should not merely
swallow all his historic Ultramontanism, but also any particular
fondness for Europe, and become Trans-oceanic.

"Moral miracles are still possible, but I have not faith to hope
for *such* a miracle as to convert in a moment the *Imperial* Church of
the City of Rome into the democratic Church of the English *world*.

"(2.) As to Socialistic changes and the position of women : these
reforms must be carried out on the democratic footing, not on the
imperialistic. As to her sympathies and history, the Roman
Church has amid the Circles of the Perfect Life in the Clerical
world endeavoured, not without magnificent successes, to realise
Socialism, and to grant to woman an equal place with man. Nun
has been equal to Monk. Princesses and Abbesses wield equal
authority to Priors and Abbots. It is easy for Rome to promote
Socialism and Woman's equality within the artificial world of
Clerical life, of (vowed) poverty and of celibacy ; but in the real
world she could not do so unless she were totally to abandon her
historic attitude. She might give instruction as to Social reform,
but chiefly by way of warning from her conventual experience. To
cease extolling celibacy as the higher state, to cease deprecating,
thereby, home life, would be to abandon her historic distinction
between lay and cleric. To give up this fundamental distinction
would be to become Protestant.

"The object of your mission seems to ask that in a moment, or
even in a generation, the absolutist Pope should become Protestant,
Puritan, Independent, Anglo-democratic, Anglo-social-democratic,
and finally, by according full equality to woman, should assert the
sovereign rights of the personal soul.

C

"To go to Rome to seek God's lever for raising the life of man is Romish, not English, and is to seek, like the Crusaders, the living Lord in an empty tomb."

My Nonconformist friend may be right. But he is, in his way, as absolutist as the Pope himself. I distrust these sweeping deductions which profess to embody the philosophy of history. It may be that, in the old Hebraic phrase, this Roman Ephraim is joined unto his idols, and that, as the Pope has been Italian and Imperialist, he will remain so to the end of time. But even in that case it may be well worth while to inquire whether it may be utterly hopeless to expect that the spirit of our age will adumbrate the uncompromising conservatism of the Vatican with the fresh and bracing air of American democracy. As for the Divine lever being this, that, and the other Church, God has so many levers, and so much need of them all, that it is never safe to ignore any, let alone one by which in times past so much of the weight of the world was raised.

I am aware that, alike to English Nonconformists, Greek Orthodox, or European Free Thinkers, I am pursuing an *ignis fatuus*. M. de Laveleye wrote to me:—

"You know nothing of the spirit of Catholicism, if you imagine that the Pope can play the *beau rôle* which you have sketched out, as a possibility of the future. Leo XIII. is before all things a diplomatist. He is dominated by a desire to re-establish the Temporal Power. To attain that end all things are made subservient. Until he renounces that dream he will be compelled to rely in the future, as in the past, upon the Governments who may help him to his goal. It was this which made him play the part of wire-puller for Prince Bismarck—a strange rôle for the representative of Christ to secure the voting of the seven years' military Budget in Germany—it was this which made him sacrifice his Poles to the Czar of Russia, and Bishop Strossmayer to the Emperor of Austria—it was this which made him pronounce in his Rescript against the cause of the tenant farmers in Ireland, and the same evil instinct nearly led him to condemn the Knights of Labour in America, if Cardinal Gibbons had not posted off to Rome just in time to avert so great a blunder. In view of all these facts, I sincerely hope that even although you have compared Cardinal Manning to St. Paul, you will not seek to place the English democracy at the feet of the Pope." M. de Laveleye does not seem to see that if he is right in his reading of the spirit of the Vatican, my admiration for Cardinal Manning, instead of leading me to the feet of the Pope, would enormously increase the force with which any English social economist and democrat would recoil from Rome. The question is, What are the facts? Whether is Cardinal Manning or M. de Laveleye the true exponent of the spirit that prevails at the capital of Catholicism?

I fully admit that if the Pope should have the courage to persevere in the path upon which he entered when he sent Cardinal Lavigerie to revive the crusade against the Slave Trade, and along which he made further progress when he supported Cardinal Manning's action in the great strike of dock labourers, he will not want for obstacles and for foes among those of his own household. Of this I had, immediately on leaving Paris, a very striking illustration. I had hardly taken my seat in the carriage at the Gare de Lyon, when I was accosted by a tall, elderly ecclesiastic by my side, who, as it turned out, was also on his way to Rome. He was a pleasant and genial travelling companion, and in the course of the run to Modane, where we parted company, we had exchanged opinions on most subjects.

He was a Doctor of Divinity,* well known in Rome, a member, as I afterwards discovered, of one of the most ancient of the religious orders of the Church, who has been for fifty years on what the Americans call " the inside track " at the Vatican. Although he had passed his seventieth year, he preserved his physical vigour, and none of the younger travellers bore so well the fatigue of the journey. The run from Paris to Rome by express train was indeed but a bagatelle to one who had first journeyed thither by a diligence, who had crossed and re-crossed the Alps scores of times before the Mount Cenis Tunnel was bored, and who remembered as if it were yesterday the immense improvement that was effected even by the mountain railway which Fell carried over the Alpine pass. My fellow-traveller was a man of masculine intelligence, with a range of

? * abbot Smith of the Benedictines."

acquaintance extending far beyond ecclesiastical circles. There were few of our English Ambassadors whom he did not know personally. He knew Mr. Gladstone, Lord Salisbury, and Lord Hartington; and although, as he repeatedly reminded me, he was only an outsider who took a distant view of English politics, all the more prominent incidents in our recent history were focussed in his mind with remarkable clearness and precision. He spoke with great freedom and intelligence upon the prospects of our Ministry, and the significance of the recent by-elections, and we were soon in the depths of a discussion as to the establishment of diplomatic relations between the Vatican and the English Government.

"The Pope," said he, "is very displeased with England, because of its refusal to enter into relations with him. There is not any day in which we do not come into contact with England at some part of the world. To-day it is in Ireland, yesterday it was in India, to-morrow it may be in Canada. But wherever it happens, there is no one with whom the Pope can speak who stands for England. It is a perpetual irritation, a constant inconvenience. Nearly every English statesman to whom I have spoken admits that it would be advantageous to have some one to represent your country at the Vatican; but as one of them said to me after admitting that it was desirable, 'English Governments can never forget that they are living practically under a régime of universal suffrage.'

The fact is, I suppose there is no party strong enough to dare to make a change which all admit to be advantageous for fear of a popular outcry." I explained to him that the objection which weighed with us was not so much the Protestant prejudice to which he attached too much importance, as the political objection to anything that seemed likely to give substance to the dream of re-establishing the temporal power, and the religious objection taken by the Irish bishops, and therefore by the Irish members, to anything that increased the power of the English Government over the head of the Church. "But," was the instant retort of my Roman doctor, "do you not see what an enormous advantage it would be for England to enter into such relations with the Pope as would enable you to prevent the appointment of any Irish bishops who were hostile to the Government? Do you think that, if you had had a fully accredited representative at the Vatican, you would ever have had Dr. Walsh as Archbishop of Dublin?"

I felt rather sick, I confess, with this cynical way of putting it. What? Had it come to this, that any one at Rome, which in her early prime had defied all the Powers and principalities of this world in order to preserve intact and unimpaired the exclusive right of selecting as bishops of the flock the men whom she considered most faithful, was now ready even to press upon an heretical Government the right of veto in exchange for this poisonous mess of diplomatic

pottage? "Give me a Nuncio at the Court of St.
James's, and I will give you in return an effective veto
upon the choice of the Irish bishops;" is it not a
compact and concrete blasphemy? Were it indeed
to be entertained by the Pope—which, of course, I
would not for a moment suppose—he would indeed
have become not the Shepherd, but the Schnadhorst
of his flock. The transaction so coolly pressed
upon me as the only statesmanlike course by this
ecclesiastic seemed to come as near the sin of
simony, in which spiritual gifts are bartered for
material advantages, as that which led Peter to tell
the original sorcerer of Samaria that he was in the
gall of bitterness and the bond of iniquity. My
companion, of course, only spoke for himself; but if
there be many like unto my interlocutor at Rome,
then, indeed, a progressive and popular Pope will find
his path impeded at every turn.

After remarking that it might be convenient for
England, but it was not surprising that the Irish
people should object to see Mr. Balfour vested with
a veto on the nomination of their bishops, I ventured
to suggest that, after all, the difficulty about the
Nuncio proved that the real centre of power,
nowadays, lay not in the Government but in the
people. "You say yourself that Ministers would
meet the wishes of the Pope, but they fear the
opposition of the people. Clearly, then, it would be
much more to the point if the Holy See were to be

in communication with the people than with the Government. And on this account a competent newspaper correspondent would be much more useful to the Pope than any Nuncio." My Roman doctor replied disdainfully, "The Press ! Rome has never used the Press, and never will. Rome has her own methods, and the Press is not among them. Believe me," he added, with a touch of pride, "we know a thing or two in Rome." The conversation passed on to Home Rule. "Home Rule," said he, "means separation. A desire for separation was the inspiring motive of the movement of 1848. It is the *arrière pensée* of the Parnellite movement to-day. Were I an English statesman I would never, never consent to the dismemberment of my country." "Of course not," I said, "and we shall never consent to it; no, not although it should be necessary to make a clean sweep of the whole population of Ireland. But we shall give them Home Rule after next general election, in order to avoid any such desperate alternative." From Home Rule, by a natural transition, we passed to the dockers' strike. It was soon evident that this good man regarded Cardinal Manning's conduct with very modified admiration. "I cannot understand," he said, "how it was that your Government stood silent by and allowed 100,000 men to march in tumultuous procession through the streets of London. Suppose that they had burned the city, what remedy would you have had ?" I gazed at him with amazement. "Yes," he continued,

" no doubt the Government had not the power; but why
did it not summon Parliament to grant it the power
necessary to disperse these processions? What power
could control so vast a mob? Who could answer for
the safety of the city? They could have expressed
their grievances in less tumultuous fashion," and so
forth, and so forth. "How long is it," I asked, "since
you were last in England?" "I have not been there
for fifty years," he replied. "I think, then, it is about
time you visited a country where men have learned that
public order rests more firmly upon the general sense of
fair play and respect for popular liberty than upon the
mere bayonets of the soldiery." We had much more
conversation, in which he told me that he was one of the
consultors of the Holy Office, which is charged with
jurisdiction over all matters of faith and morals; that
his board, which is composed of Cardinals alone, had
power to place any book on the Index, "even if it were
written by a cardinal and commended by the Pope," he
said, somewhat significantly. I have since learned that
he is often told off to meet distinguished strangers as
the representative of the Vatican. He said that Rome
represented before all the world the principle of authority. I sincerely hope that he does not really represent
Rome. If he does, Heaven help Rome! It was difficult to imagine that such a man should feel himself at
home in a Church which has a Manning and Moran
and Gibbons among its cardinals, and Walsh and Croke
and Ireland among its archbishops, and much more

difficult to think that he could enjoy the confidence of
the Holy See. It was, I suppose, such men as he,
whose utter inability to realise the power that resides
in liberty, whose blindness to every principle but that of
material force, led Mazzini to address the Œcumenical
Council in the famous passage in which he tells them :—

"Disinherited alike of inspiration and affection, having abdi-
cated all power of intervention in events that transform and
improve God's earth, you who were once the world's centre are
gradually being driven back to its extremest orbit, and are destined
to find yourselves at last alone in the void beyond. Motionless
sphinxes in the vast desert; you inertly contemplate the shadows of
the centuries as they pass. Humanity, whom you should have
guided, has gone otherwhere."

It was a good thing, no doubt, for me at the very
inception of my inquiries to be brought into close
contact with a spirit so absolutely opposed to the mind
that is in Cardinal Manning. Of course, in myself my
travelling companion proves nothing. He may be a
white blackbird, or rather a black swan, among the
ecclesiastics of the Curia. Exceptions prove the rule,
and the presence of one bigoted reactionary in any
institution is no evidence as to its unprogressive
character. But it would be idle to deny that, among
those outside the Church with whom I have spoken,
there is a general concurrence of opinion that I shall
find that he is much more in accord with the prevailing
spirit at the Vatican than is Cardinal Manning. A
fervid and conscientious Catholic layman said to me,
" It is Bishop Vaughan rather than Cardinal Manning

who represents the temper of the Papal Court. The
views which shocked you so much on the part of your
travelling companion are held and expressed with diplomatic modifications by the highest personages around
the Pope. When Leo XIII. expressed his readiness to
receive Mr. Gladstone last December against the protest
of Monsignor Stonor, he based his decision not on the
attempts which Mr. Gladstone had made to pacify
Ireland, nor on his position as an English statesman, but
because he believed him to be the first English Minister
who had endeavoured to establish direct diplomatic
communication between England and Rome. Captain
Ross, of Bladensburg, an Irish landlord born in Italy, to
whom the Duke of Norfolk was a mere figurehead, has
more influence with the Pope than all the Irish bishops
put together."

This was put far more strongly by an American
observer, who has a wide experience of Churches and
religion in both hemispheres, and who for many years
has made a close study of men and things at the Vatican.
He said: "If you want to find real religious life in the
Catholic Church, Rome is the last place in which to seek
for it. The Church is like a great banyan tree, which
has thrown out vigorous branches that have taken root
in all the countries round about. They are alive, but
the parent trunk is dead. Religious faith has died out
of the Italian mind. This great religious machine is run
by the least religious minds in the whole communion.
They are astute, acute, diplomatic, and full of all the

resources of statecraft. But religion, in the sense in
which Catholics understand it in England, in Ireland,
in America, in Germany, and even in France, is
simply non-existent for them. They are indifferent to
those things. If there is to be a great revival of Catholicism, it will begin where men believe, not where they
merely engineer the machine. To them authority is the
governing principle, and they lay a stress upon this
which is fatal to progress. If Cardinal Manning or Cardinal Gibbons were to be made Pope to-morrow, they
would be unable to change the attitude of the Church.
The power of the individual Pontiff is infinitesimal, compared with the fossilised influence of centuries. Pio Nono
tried it, and the result of his experiment intensified the
Conservatism of the Curia. The revolution which ex-
pelled him from Rome is regarded as decisive against
any further dealings with Liberalism. In a hundred
years the world will speak English, no doubt, and if you
made your language phonetic, the change would come in
half that time; but has even a glimmering of that fact
penetrated the Italian mind? The world is becoming
Democratic—Socialistic, if you please—but the Holy
See still seeks its alliances among the Princes, and not
among the Peoples. And as for your third inquiry
about the relation of the Holy See to the emancipation
of women, it is vain to dream of a revolution which
would cut up by the roots the one hold which the
Church has upon mankind. If it were not for the
prejudices instilled into men when still children at their

mothers' knees, where would Catholicism be to-day?
Give women the intelligence of men, and you dry up
Catholicism at its fount. You can hardly expect any
help from the Pope in that enterprise."

I quote without endorsing the pessimism of my
American informant, in order to bring into clear relief
the prevailing opinion as to the antagonism which is
supposed to exist between Catholicism as it is understood by Manning and Walsh, and Catholicism as it is
embodied in many of those who surround the Pope.
One thing is evident. If there be even but a modicum
of truth in these opinions, so far from regarding the
banishment of the Pope from Rome as a calamity, it is
a consummation devoutly to be desired by every believer
in the Divine mission of a Church which, if it is ever to
be Catholic, must, in the real sense of that term,
assuredly cease to be Italian.

CHAPTER IV.

THE POPE'S ASPIRATIONS.

In Europe there are at this moment but three men who stand out above their fellows as the supreme representatives of various kinds of power. Alexander the Third represents the authority of material force, Prince Bismarck the might of scientific organisation, and Leo the Thirteenth the strength of the Catholic world. Of the three the Pope is the most interesting and autocratic. His empire is vaster than that of the Russian Tzar, and before his authority even the imperious Chancellor has been compelled to bow. Although a prisoner in his own palace, he is ruler of a dominion as wide as the world, and there is no language spoken among men wherein his word is not recognised as the voice of a master. There is a loneliness and a mystery about Leo that differentiates him from the other potentates of our day. Prince Bismarck is intensely human. He stands before us as the very incarnation of masterful man. He lives before us, complete in all human relations, with his wife, his sister, his sons, his dogs, his pipe, and his beer; he touches the common life of his day at every point. It is the same with the Tzar: although in his case he is more withdrawn from the public gaze, he shares not less fully the ordinary life of the ordinary man. As father, as husband, as master, as friend, he is a man among men; nor does the burden of empire separate him from the simple family joys and natural every-day cares of the human home. But the Pope stands apart. He sleeps as other men, and eats as they, but a great gulf yawns between him and other mortals. He has a palace, but he is without a home. He has servants and domestic friends; but the celibacy which for centuries has been imposed upon the clergy of his Church debars him from the deepest and most human of all relationships. He has never known the joys nor suffered the sorrows which make up a great part of the higher life of the ordinary man. He has lived and lives apart, alone, divorced from nature, that he may be consecrated to the service of his Church, without wife or child, that he may care solely for the Bride of the Lamb, and watch more sedulously over the welfare of those who are of the household of faith.

The Pope, thus excluded from the healthy human life of the family, clings all the more passionately to the local surroundings which serve him as a substitute for home. His centre is not a home. It is Rome. The result is that the disadvantages which celibacy was established to avert reappear in another shape. He that is married careth for the things that are of the world—how he may please his wife; whereas he that is unmarried careth for the things that belong to the Lord, how he may please the Lord. For the world and the wife, read Rome and its sovereignty, and it is equally true of the Popes. The local anxieties, the temporal government of the city in which the Popes succeeded the Cæsars, have become as cramping and crippling to the successors of St. Peter as the household cares that might have encompassed them had they all imitated the Fisherman, who, at one time of his life, had not only a wife, but a mother-in-law. It is this which gives such strange interest to the position of Leo the Thirteenth at the present moment. He is distracted between conflicting ideals—exactly as a good father of a family is often torn asunder between the claims of his household and the claims of the world at large. The struggle which is going on in the Vatican is but the latest phase of the conflict which the apostle declared troubled the married man who had to reconcile the desire to please the Lord with the desire to please his wife.

As some men never have any divine call that leads them to discharge duties outside their own doorstep, so some Popes have never recognised the existence of duties incompatible with their primary fealty to the local interests of the Italian town in which they have spent their lives. That which distinguishes Leo the Thirteenth is that before his mind there has passed a vision of a higher and nobler ideal than that of being the mere temporal master of the Eternal City. He has seen, as it were in a dream, a vision of a wider sovereignty than any which the greatest of his predecessors had ever realised, and before his eyes there has been unfolded a

magnificent conception of a really universal Church.
But no sooner has he gazed with holy ecstasy on the
world-wide dominion which lies almost within his grasp,
than he turns with a sigh to the older and smaller ideal
of the temporal sovereignty of Rome, which has bounded
the horizon of so many of his predecessors, and which
presses upon him like the atmosphere of the whole of his
waking life. These are the two dreams, the two ideals,
hopelessly antagonistic one to the other: but Leo help-
lessly clings to both.

To those who do not look at the world and its affairs
from an out-of-the-way corner of the world from which
the tide of Empire has long since ebbed, it is difficult to
see how any comparison can be made between the two
ideals which haunt the imagination of the Holy Father.
It is, to put it vulgarly, all Lombard Street to a China
orange in favour of the world-wide ideal. And yet
there is to those who have been born and bred under
Italian skies a strong and natural fascination about the
ideal which centres in the re-establishment of Papal
sovereignty in Rome. Rome is a name to conjure with.
For more than two thousand years the Seven-hilled City
was for weal or for woe more important than any other
point in the world's surface. It is the only city which
ever conquered a continent. Alike as the seat of the
Republic, of the Empire, and of the Popedom of the
Middle Ages, Rome was the capital of the world. The
broad arrow of Roman Empire is branded deep on the
body of our civilisation. Our law, our language, our

D

habits, our religion—all have the impress of the Roman mint. The very air of Europe is impregnated with the ozone that streams, as from a perennial fountain, from the history of Rome. There is everything that can fascinate the imagination and stimulate the mind in the traditions that cling round the ruined walls of the Eternal City ; nor can the least reverent be unconscious of the awe excited by the sacred shrines which for a thousand years have absorbed the devotion of the world.

> " Mother of Arts as once of Arms ; thy hand
> Was then our guardian, and is still our Guide.
> Parent of our religion ! "

To reign in Rome might well rouse the loftiest ambition, and to lose the sovereignty of the Imperial City might rend the heart of the most callous of mortals. That great city which reigneth over the kings of the earth, and below whose feet St. John saw peoples, and multitudes, and nations and tongues, was, at any time between the days of the Scipios and the era of the Medici, the natural centre of any organisation that sought to exercise world-wide dominion. Civilisation grew up round the shores of the Mediterranean, that inland sea which was the cradle of the culture of the world. To a devout Catholic, not even the sacred sites which witnessed the passion of our Lord are more sacred than the city where the first martyrs, swathed in pitchy cerements, blazed as torches in the gardens of Nero, and where their descendants founded an empire more splendid than that of Augustus, more beneficent than that of the Antonines. The City of the Catacombs and of the Coliseum, where generation after generation of the most divinely gifted of our race have lavished the utmost resources of their art, their intellect, and their genius, may well seem marked out from of old to be the natural and eternal seat of the Vicegerent of God.

Apart from these considerations, which appeal to all men, the Roman Pontiffs have acquired in the course of ages, by mere force of inveterate habit, an instinct which renders it almost impossible for them to conceive of a Catholic Church which has not Rome as its centre. Use and wont are great deities even in the spiritual realm, and use and wont point to Rome and Rome alone as the centre of the Catholic world. Many a time the Popes have been driven from Rome: sometimes they have voluntarily left it: but sooner or later they have always returned to it. The administration of the most gigantic polity known to man is centralised there. All roads lead to Rome, and from Rome there have issued since Christian civilisation began the winged words of power and of life which have knit the Catholic world into one.

It is therefore natural that the Pope should cling to Rome, and should regard a possible retreat to Malta as but a temporary flight from a passing storm. Some day the sky will clear, and once more the Vicar of Christ will re-occupy the See of St.

Peter. Equally natural is it that, being in Rome, he should wish to be master in his own house. Absolute independence is an indispensable condition for the free exercise of the spiritual power. This independence, according to English ideas, can best be obtained by the abandonment by the spiritual power of all temporal claims, and the recognition by the secular government that it has no authority in the spiritual realm. But this ideal, which can be realised where there is no antagonism between Church and State, is manifestly impossible where, as in Italy, the State is practically a rival Church, almost as determined to persecute as Torquemada or Calvin. Hence to the Pope it seems as part of the ordinance of God that he should dwell in Rome, and, being resident there, that he should reign in the Eternal City as its temporal lord; not because he cares for the sceptre of secular dominion, but because nothing short of sovereignty can, under the circumstances, secure him the freedom necessary for the exercise of his spiritual prerogatives. It is this which dominates the mind of Leo the Thirteenth. Waking or sleeping, the idea of restoring the lost temporal dominion of his predecessors never leaves him. It colours the whole texture of his thoughts, it influences his policy, and makes itself felt throughout the whole orbit of Pontifical action.

And here it may be observed in passing that, however absorbing may be the influence of Roman politics on the Holy See at the present moment, when the restoration of its temporal sovereignty is but a theory or an aspiration, it is nothing to the distraction that would follow if the Pope were to be cursed with the burden of a granted prayer, and set up once more on the throne of Rome.

This, however, by the way. The Pope does not realise the truth, and the re-establishment of his temporal sovereignty is still his first dream, a dream of the dear dead past, hallowed no doubt by innumerable sacred associations, but limited, local, and fatally opposed to the realisation of his other dream, which intermittently exercises a very powerful influence over his imagination. This second vision is infinitely more sublime than the restitution of the unimpaired sovereignty of the Papal See over all the ancient patrimony of the Church. Leo has dreamed of being really the Pastor of the world, in fact as well as in name. To be Vicegerent of God, and therefore representative of the Father of all men, is to stand *in loco parentis* to all the human race. The Church, the Lamb's Bride, is the mother of humanity. As head of the Church, he must care with a mother's love for all the children of the family. It matters not that many are orphaned from birth, knowing not of their divine parentage. It is for him to teach them of the Fatherhood of God, and to prove to them by infinite acts of helpful service the reality of the motherhood of the Church. No difference of creed, no blindness of negation, no obstinacy of unbelief, can shut out any human soul from the loving care of the shepherd to whom God has entrusted the guardianship of His flock.

Humanity wanders in the wilderness: he will be its guide. The forces of evil abound, making sad havoc of the forlorn children of men : he will stand in the breach, and cast the shield of divine grace and of human service over the victims of the Evil One. Men are ignorant: he will teach them. They are groping in the dark: he will lead them into light. Up from the void everywhere rises a despairing cry, Who will show us any good? And from the recesses of the Vatican palace he answers, " I will conduct you into the paths of all peace."

This, of course, or something like this, has ever been the aspiration of all the greater Popes. But Leo differs from his predecessors in being more under the influence of the modern spirit, which has read a more mundane meaning into the words of Christ. It is reported of Anaxagoras that, in his old age, having abandoned all interest in the politics of his time, he was reproached for ceasing to care for his country. " Be silent," he replied; " I have the greatest affection for my country," pointing upwards as he spoke to the stars. It is in exactly the opposite direction that Leo has moved. No doubt, like all Christians, he would say that he set not his affections on things below, but on things above—that here he had no continuing city, but had a house eternal in the heavens; but that is no longer the note of Christian thought. Rather does he pray with our Lord, " Thy kingdom come, Thy will be done on earth as it is in heaven;" and in his vision of things to come he sees the kingdoms of the earth become the Lord's and his

Christ's. It is to establish the City of God in the hearts and the lives of men, not in the future or beyond the grave, but here and now, that he has been called to the Papal throne. Not from any mere lust of power and personal ambition, but with a genuine aspiration to be helpful to mankind, Leo dreams of re-establishing on a wider basis and a surer foundation the spiritual authority of Innocent the Third and of Gregory the Seventh. He feels himself called to make the Holy See once more the active and omnipresent embodiment of the conscience of mankind. He is to be the organ through which God speaks, not merely concerning dogmas as to the divine attributes, or in defining differences between orthodox and heretical subtleties, but as the living guide, the lively oracle from which all the races of mankind may derive the same practical and authoritative counsel that the Hebrews obtained from the Urim and the Thummim of their high priest. Leo would fain be the Moses of the new Exodus of Humanity, their leader through the Wilderness of Sin to the Promised Land, in which all the evils of the existing society will be done away, and all things political and social will have become new.

Leo the Thirteenth is, in short, a Pope who takes himself seriously, who believes in his divine mission, and who is penetrated by the conviction that the Church must address herself practically to the solution of all the pressing problems of life. *Homo sum, nihil humanum a me alienum puto*, takes with him a wider and nobler

range.   He is not merely a man among men, but representative of the God who hath made of one blood all
nations of men for to dwell on all the face of the earth ;
therefore he must interest himself in every department
of human life.   All this, which may seem to some but
as the wildest lunacy, and to others as insufferable
arrogance, has indeed a very solid foundation.   Whatever may be said against the Catholic Church, it does
unquestionably represent an immense moral force.   The
most bigoted Protestant may therefore rejoice at the
prospect of this moral force being directed to practical
ends.   Hitherto, unquestionably, the Popes have not
lived up to their privileges, and very few of them have
even attempted to rise to the level of their opportunities.
If Leo the Thirteenth is really about to apply the vast
moral force of which he is the official embodiment to
the solution of the practical questions of the day, even
those who are most sceptical about the supernatural
grace on which he bases his claim may well rejoice that
so vast a moral influence is no longer to be wasted on
what they cannot but regard as theological puerilities
and ecclesiastical trifles.

   But, alas ! the moment the Pope essays to make a
step towards the realisation of his world-wide ideal, he
seems to be checked and thwarted by his earlier dream !
When he would act as the conscience of mankind, he is
in danger of being biassed by his aspiration to be an
Italian prince.   When he attempts to set up a supreme
tribunal for the guidance of humanity, the Italian limita-

times are apt to baffle him; and instead of being cosmopolitan, catholic, and impartial, he is tempted to become
Roman, local, and partisan. If he is really to rise to the
height of his greater ideal, he will have to make up his
mind to sacrifice the smaller. If he would spread his
wings over the whole world, he must desist from
attempting to creep back into his Roman chrysalis.
The new Moses will not make much of a success of his
Exodus if he is perpetually struggling to get back to the
flesh-pots of Egypt.

A very interesting picture might be drawn of the
daily life of the Pope in his palace-prison. In some
respects it must be admitted that the spectacle is almost
ideal. Imagine a pure, good, and able man, of more
than threescore years and ten, rising at six o'clock on
any given morning, after a sleep as untroubled as a
child's, and setting about what is in his own honest conviction the discharge of his duty to God and His
Church, by using his influence as the Vicegerent of the
Almighty to allay the troubles of the world. His authority,
to begin with, is almost absolutely untrammelled. When
Alexander the Third writes, he uses M. de Giers as a
pen. Cardinal Rampolla is equally the pen of Leo the
Thirteenth. Around the Papal throne are Cardinals,
and Archbishops, and dignitaries of great place; but in
all the brilliant throng there is no one who exercises any
controlling influence over the detached and lucid
intellect of the Pope. Occasionally, earlier in his reign,
they would endeavour to bring pressure to bear to

induce him to adopt a policy to which he was disinclined. "What you say," he would reply, "is very good, no doubt, but let it be done in a different way." And done it always was in Leo's way, until at last the Cardinals desisted from making fruitless suggestions. He is so supreme that, compared with the elevation which he occupies, Cardinals count for no more than deacons or even than acolytes. There are mutterings of discontent in the Congregations from men who once counted for something in the Church, but now count for nothing; but on the whole the Sacred College recognises with loyalty and pride the commanding ability and authoritative confidence of its chief. The Pope, therefore, has a single mind, and he has an immense sense of his responsibility for the decisions at which he arrives. Every morning, before addressing himself to the direction of the affairs of this planet, he offers the sacrifice of the Mass, and then for *gratiarum actio* attends a second Mass, at which his chaplain is the celebrant. With a mind thus attuned to divine things, the Pope then begins his working day. A single glass of coffee, tea, or milk suffices to break his fast. After going through his papers, he begins to receive about nine. From that hour till one in the afternoon the throng of visitors never slackens. Secretaries, Ambassadors, Cardinals from the Congregation, distinguished strangers, Bishops from afar, have audience in turn. There are 1,200 bishops in the Catholic Church, and with all of them the Pope is in more or less constant personal relations. Nothing can be more gracious, more animated, or more sympathetic than the manner of the Pope. His eye, which when fixed in thought is deep and piercing, beams with kindliness, and the severely rigid lines of his intellectual features relax with the pleasantest of smiles as he talks, using, as the case may be, either French, Latin (which he speaks with great purity and facility), or his own musical native tongue. After four or five hours spent in this way, he returns to his papers and his books until three, when he dines. His meal is frugal: a little soup, two courses of meat with vegetables, and dessert of fruit, with one glass of strong wine, suffice for his wants. After dinner he goes out for a drive or a walk in the gardens of the Vatican. In the evening he resumes his papers, and at night between nine and ten all the Papal household assemble for the Rosary, after which they retire to rest. But long after that hour the Cardinal State Secretary, Rampolla, or the Under-State Secretary, Mocenni, is often summoned to the Papal apartments, where, by the light of the midnight lamp, Leo watches and thinks and prays for the welfare of the Church.

Here, if anywhere on the world's surface, it might be thought, was to be found a tribunal removed far from the distractions of this world, and a judge fully aware of the enormous responsibility which presses with undivided force upon the supreme representative of the Christian conscience.

The Pope, on the two occasions on which I had an

opportunity of observing him closely, impressed me very favourably. There is in the actual face nothing of that sly smirk which appears in almost all of his photographs. There is a genial benevolence in his countenance and a twinkle of humour in his bright eye. Although he is apt to be bored by the endless string of solemn triflers who are presented on the days when he gives audience, it is a weariness of the mind rather than a weariness of the body. During the celebration of his Jubilee he wearied out all the younger men who were in attendance at his Court. "The Pope is seventy-nine," said one of them, "but do not deceive yourself by the almanack. He is as vigorous in mind and almost as alert in body as if he were only fifty." This is no doubt an exaggeration, but it represents the honest impression of one who is in a position to contrast the physical endurance of Leo XIII. with that of the younger men who surrounded him. He did not seem to me decrepit or infirm. His old schoolfellow, Monsignor Kirby, Archbishop of Ephesus, who discharges the responsible duties of Rector of the Irish College without any trace of senile infirmity, is six years the senior of the Pope. Allowance, no doubt, must be made for the superior vitality of the Irish stock; but it would be a mistake to regard Leo XIII. as tottering on the edge of the grave. He has the *mens sana in corpore sano;* and as long as he lives there will not fail, to the guidance of the Church, the intellect of a statesman and the heart of a saint.

Cardinal Rampolla, the Secretary of State, the Pope's

right hand, who occupies rooms in the Vatican immediately above the Papal apartments, impressed me most favourably. He has the manners of a prince, the courtesy of a diplomatist, and the quick, penetrating intelligence of a modern statesman. He is an Italian, and a southern Italian. But he is candid and frank, and in our conversations I always felt that I was talking to a genuine man, who liked to come straight to the point, and who did not fool away his time over nonsense. He was, perhaps, a little given to the tricks of fence natural to the diplomatist; but after a while, when you got to close quarters with the real man, all that went by the board. He is not a fanatic in any sense, any more than is Lord Dufferin, whom in the charm of his manner he somewhat resembles; but he is well spoken of as a good man by those who know him, he is trusted by the Pope, and he is quite enough man of the world to be competent to fill his present post. Above all, he is young, the youngest Cardinal, I believe, but one in the Sacred College. He is only forty-five, and looks even younger.

Monsignor Jacobini is the coming man at the Propaganda. If I only could feel sure that he was not putting more strain upon his strength than it can support, I should be inclined to augur that in him was the most promising hope for the immediate future of the Church. But he overworks constantly, and he does so knowing that his hold on life is by no means so tenacious as his friends could desire. If any one could induce Monsignor

Jacobini to take more care of himself, that person should deserve a high place among the benefactors of the Church. Cardinal Parocchi who, as the Vicar-General of the Pope, apart from the possibilities of his selection by the next conclave, must rank among the leading personalities of Rome, is undoubtedly shrewd and able; and although heroic altruism can hardly be regarded as the dominant note of his career, I was most agreeably surprised to find him so much more in sympathy with the spirit of the times than I had anticipated. I had feared to have found him a Roman Pobedonestzeff. He is at the worst only an Italian Sir William Harcourt.

Monsignor Mocenni, the Under-Secretary of State, the man who, after Cardinal Rampolla, comes most into personal contact with the Pope, is a thoroughly honest man, an indefatigable worker, and personally popular among the Papal staff. He suffers from asthma; but this, although a sore drain upon his nervous energy, never is allowed to interfere with the discharge of duty. I found him personally courteous, but as unsympathetic as a great permanent under-secretary in Downing Street would be were he suddenly to be startled by a premature call from Macaulay's New Zealander, who came to ask what should be done with the ruins of St. Paul's. It has been said of Anglican bishops that they tend inevitably to degenerate into great overgrown clerks, and Monsignor Mocenni is a victim of the same circumstances. He has all the ciphers to decipher, and all the routine of the business of the Vatican passes through his hands. He has to be ready at any hour of the day or night to answer the Pope's call, and supply him with the documents or information which he requires. Like any man in such a position, he is apt to regard all things which increase friction as if they were necessarily evil instead of being symptoms of growing vitality. The Irish question, for instance, is a troublesome encrescence foreign to the work of the Church, and a horrible bore to the Secretary of State's office. Ireland, after all, matters very little to an office where "the Truth about the Roman Question" can be offered to an inquirer as summing up all the information which any one can possibly want at the Vatican, and as it matters little it is not understood. It is quite natural that such a man in such a position should be tempted to regard all the Irish bishops—of course excepting the Abdiel of Limerick—as more or less of contumacious rebels, and it is equally natural that he should be regarded by the Irish as an incarnation of Castle Government established at the Vatican. If the Pope would make Monsignor Mocenni Metropolitan of the Cannibal Islands, and insist upon his taking up his residence in his new diocese, great would be the joy among the Irish sons of the Holy Father; for Monsignor Mocenni cannot even in conversation listen without horror to the mere suggestion that possibly the Pope has made more than one mistake in the treatment of the Irish question.

I have purposely dealt with the men who are at the top before attempting to summarise the net result of what they told me. For character counts for so much that we can look forward with much more confidence to the future if we have confidence in the heads and hearts of the men who, to use an expressive Americanism, run the machine, than we could merely because for the moment these views seemed to us wise or the reverse.

CHAPTER V.

I STOOD the other night upon a balcony of the Vatican, and looked down from the palace of the Popes over the city of the Cæsars. It was an impressive scene, and one which I witnessed for the first time, but which is constantly visible to the Pope. Above, the black violet of the sky of the Italian night was as yet faintly gemmed with stars; and far below, spreading over its more than seven hills, lay the Imperial city, everywhere gleaming with gas, and here and there radiant with the electric light. All was still in the precincts of the great palace, save for the occasional tread of the halberdier, whose picturesque uniform framed itself at times with strange mediæval quaintness in the fire-lit gateway. On the right rose the mighty dome of St. Peter, towering huge into the silent sky. Below ran the yellow Tiber, beyond which stretched the crowded streets, busy with the hum and murmur of a nation's capital, and the great outlines of the domes and towers of the innumerable churches of Rome. It was the Nineteenth Century spread out at the feet of the Fourteenth, while beyond and above them both towered the vast and cloudy shades of other

E

centuries, whose sons made Rome immortal.   Standing at the door of the Secretary of State's office, I
recalled the conversation I had had within ; and as I
looked down from my coign of vantage on the distant
lines of lamps that etched in outlines of light the extent
of Rome, it seemed to recall the familiar story of the
Temptation in the Wilderness.   From some such lofty
height it was that the tempter showed Jesus of Nazareth
all the kingdoms of the world and the glory of them,
saying, " All these things will I give thee, if thou wilt
fall down and worship me."   There was the city—

> " Great and glorious Rome, queén of the Earth,
>   So far renowned, and with the spoils enrich'd
>   Of nations ; "

and there, across the courtyard in his stately palace-
prison, was the man whose proudest title is that of Vicar
of the Nazarene.   Constantly before him is the temptation.   Constantly at his elbow whispers the tempter :
" All this will I give thee—temporal sovereignty, and
independence, and rule over all this city—if thou wilt
fall down and worship me."   It is the Temptation of the
Wilderness renewed in our time ; a temptation that has
not passed, and will not pass.   It is now in an acute
form, for Rome is still full of French Pilgrims, acclaim-
ing "The Pope-King;" and the hopes of the Faithful are
stirred within them at the thought that perhaps next
year, or, if not then, the year after, the Pope will have
his own again, and the successor of St. Peter may once
more reign in majesty on the throne of the Cæsars.

This spectacle is, I confess, far more intensely
interesting to me than all the painted canvas and
plaster in Roman museums and churches, whereby
inspired painters have endeavoured to portray the
familiar incidents of sacred story. For here is no
painting of what happened long ago. Here is the
actual temptation in all its grim and terrible reality,
with all the forces of evil arrayed against the frail and
half-overpowered resistance of a good but aged Pope.
The temptation so constantly present is that of hoping
for a foreign war that might result in the re-establishment of the Temporal Power. Before that temptation
many of those around the Pope have long ago succumbed. They are on their faces before the tempter;
their secret thoughts are but so many prayers for his
speedy advent; and if they could but have their way
they would, in Mr. Gladstone's lurid phrase, not hesitate
to re-establish the Temporal Power, even if it could be
only done by setting up the terrestrial throne of the
Popedom on the ashes of the city, and amidst the
whitening bones of its people. But the Pope is a good
man, a sincere Christian, whose heart overflows with
sympathy for the human race. The temptation comes
to him, as temptations always come to higher natures,
so veiled, that it seems almost a prompting from the
very Spirit of God. The tempter is disguised as an
angel of light. No mean, or sordid, or worldly motives
weigh with the good Pope as he stands at the windows
of the Vatican and looks out over the Imperial City to

the darkening slopes of the Sabine Hills, and sighs at
the thought that the unification of his country has been
purchased at the price of the spoliation of his Church.
What he thinks of is not the petty power of presiding
over the construction of the drains, or the absorbing
duty of organising the police of the city out of which he
is now a voluntary outcast.   He believes, with the
honest sincerity of conviction natural to an aged ecclesiastic born and bred in the Pontifical States, that it is
practically impossible for the Catholic Church throughout the world to be administered by one who is not an
independent sovereign.   The man at the helm of the
Church must not be the subject of any mortal.   The
Vicar of Christ must not be called upon to bow to the
decrees of a mongrel Cæsar.   Hence he has convinced
himself that he must get back his temporal sovereignty
if the government of the Church is not to go to pieces.
That is with him, not unnaturally, considering his years
and his education, an axiom which he does not discuss.
He starts from that, and always reverts to it.   But here
before his eyes is unfolded day by day the triumphant
demonstration by his enemies of the fact that the temporal sovereignty has passed away.   The king sits in
the palace which the Popes occupied on the Quirinal;
the departments of the Italian State are installed in
buildings once sacred to the offices of the Church; the
midday gun which is fired every day is served by Italian
gunners from his own castle of San Angelo, where they
are constructing balloons for the Abyssinian war; and

great barracks, crowded with soldiers, where the bugle call sounds incessant, stand almost within hail of the Vatican. Day by day, year in, year out, the august prisoner never opens his eyes at daybreak without longing that the new day might bring deliverance; and the shades of night never blot the great panorama of the city from his gaze that he does not cry, in the agony of a heart sick by hope deferred. "How long, O Lord, how long?"

In 1889 the iron entered more deeply into his soul than ever, owing to the erection of a monument to Giordano Bruno in the market-place, where the heresiarch was burnt nearly 300 years ago. No incident of late years has so deeply wounded the sentiments of the rulers of the Church as the unveiling of that monument on June 9. The Inquisition had burned Bruno in 1600; and although the Church might have ignored the tribute paid to his memory, that was not the spirit in which the Bruno celebration was treated by the Vatican. The Pentecostal Festival was clouded by a gloom that could be felt. The whole Church was invited to share in the indignation with which its head regarded the sacrilege of the commemoration, and in every way the Pope made all men understand that the iron had entered into his soul. He spent the whole day in his private chapel, prostrate before the Blessed Sacrament exposed on the altar, praying in the midst of the assembled prelates of his Court for an expiation of the blasphemies of Campo de Fiori. From Saturday till Wednesday morning no one was allowed to enter the Vatican but the Ambassadors of foreign Powers accredited to the Holy See. It was to him as if the Abomination of Desolation had been set up in the Holy of Holies, and the unveiling of a statue to the heresiarch was proclaimed to be the outward and visible sign of the determination of the triumphant Revolution to press forward to the "overthrow of the sacred authority of the Pontiffs, and the extirpation of the Christian faith."

The Sacred College of Cardinals was summoned to a most secret and extraordinary Consistory, in a form and under precautions which had only twice been adopted in the long reign of Pius the Ninth. At this Consistory Leo the Thirteenth communicated to his Cardinals the grave decision at which he had arrived. The solemn Allocution which he addressed to them, and which was subsequently published to the world, amounted practically to a Pontifical declaration that Rome was no longer a safe or tenable residence for the successor of St. Peter. The freedom of the Apostolic functions and the dignity of the Pontifical office, already impaired from of old by the usurpation of the Revolution, were now menaced with extinction by the growing insolence of the sects of evil. The daring of desperate men, unchained to every crime, driven on by the fierceness of lawless desires, could no longer be restrained; the city that was once the safe and inviolable seat of the Holy See was now the capital of a new

impiety, where absurd and impudent worship was paid
to human reason. "Hereby is rendered evident in
what condition is placed the Supreme Head of the
Church, the Pastor and the Teacher of the Catholic
world."

It is very difficult for us in England to realise the
feelings of the Pope and of his counsellors as to the
immensity of the injury which they conceive has been
inflicted upon the Church by the occupation of Rome.
To most Englishmen the establishment of the capital of
united Italy at Rome seemed the natural and most
desirable consummation of the national movement in
the Peninsula. In many cases religious prejudice
united with nationalist enthusiasm to blind us to the
extent to which the change was certain to wound the
Holy See. But after the lapse of nineteen years the
wound still bleeds. Not to perceive this is to fail
to understand the tragic force of the temptation to
which the Pope is subjected. To any one who
approaches the subject from the standpoint of an
English Liberal—especially from that of the English
Nonconformist, to whom the union between Church and
State, whether in England or in Rome, is more or less
anti-Christian—the very bitterness of the pain which
the Pope feels as he mourns over the loss of his
Temporal Power is a measure of the necessity for the
revolution which has torn it from his grasp. But that
sentiment is, of course, quite foreign to the mind of the
Pope, and the ideal of the Liberation Society gives him

no help in resisting the temptation to do what he can to bring about a war between Italy and France. Of course, to any one who knows what war is, and who can form an idea of the immensity of the sacrifices which the next war will entail, the suggestion that the Vicar of Christ should, for the sake of regaining the sovereignty of Rome, promote war between France and Italy, seems almost unutterably damnable. But the Pope has never seen war on any extended scale. He may not realise in his simple apartments in the Vatican how many hamlets would have to blaze heaven high, how many fields be drenched with blood, what enormous burdens would be piled upon the shoulders of the labouring poor, before even the first step could be taken towards expelling King Humbert from Rome. Besides, even if he did realise what an outpouring of the vials of the wrath of God would follow a declaration of war, the tempter at his elbow could easily present specious arguments to prove that, after all, the storm might clear the air, and that worse things might happen than that the judgments of Heaven should overtake the impious usurpers of the patrimony of St. Peter. The Holy See never hesitated in times past to call in the aid of King Pepin and his Franks. Thirty-three times, say angry patriots, have the Popes called in foreign troops to enable them to rule in Rome. And while to other rulers the precedents of their predecessors might seem merely hints which might or might not be followed, the Popes are tempted to regard each other as being more or less inspired. The whole history of the Church seems to them a series of inspired sign-posts, pointing out the path which the Pontiffs must follow. One hundred and fifty times have the Popes seen their Temporal Power seized by usurping hands, and one hundred and fifty times the Popes have regained their sceptre, often by means which, to the humanitarian moralist of the nineteenth century, seem most deplorable, but which, having been crowned by success and sanctioned by the Popes, can hardly be condemned by Leo XIII. "As your predecessors have done, so do you! Granting that great suffering may result from war, when have the Popes ever hesitated to invoke the sword of the Lord and of Gideon in the defence of the most sacred interests of the Church? And what can be more sacred than the Temporal Power, that adamantine casket in which there has been preserved for thirteen centuries the spiritual independence of the Holy See?" So whispers Mephistopheles; and poor Faust, weary with waiting for the deliverance that delayeth its coming, may be excused if now and then he turns his eyes in longing to the north, and sees in pious ecstasy the warriors of France marching down in triumph to restore him to his throne. They did it once before in his lifetime. Why may they not do it again?

When I attempted to discuss the question in the office of the Papal Secretary of State, I was assured on the highest authority but one among the officials of the Vatican that I should find the whole question dealt with in the most masterly and authoritative manner in a pamphlet which had recently been published. It was not, I was told, written by the Pope or issued by the Holy See, but it was drawn up practically under the supervision of the Papal authorities, and I could rely upon the contents of the pamphlet as being absolutely authentic. This, I was afterwards assured by a still higher authority, was an exaggeration of the facts, the pamphlet not being official or even officious, and I gladly accept the correction. But on my first visit to the Vatican the authority of the pamphlet was asserted in the strongest terms. The pamphlet, a copy of which was then handed me, is entitled "La Verità intorno alla Questione Romana," by "B. O. S." "This," I was told, "will answer all your questions, and until you read it, it would be idle to discuss anything further." The pamphlet is undoubtedly an able and very smart presentation of the case in favour of the Temporal Power. I quote one passage, which made me shudder. Speaking of the impolicy from the Italian point of view of the occupation of Rome, the author pointed out that the effect of such an action was to place in the hands of every Power a blank bill of exchange, which may be presented at any time against Italy, "the faculty that is," says the author of the pamphlet, "given into the hands of every Power of attacking Italy as often as is convenient to them under colour of religion *being applauded not only by the Catholic subjects of the country but by every Catholic in the world.*" Now here un-

doubtedly is a complete surrender on the part of the
author of the pamphlet to the tempter. So far is he
from thinking that a declaration of war against Italy for
the sake of establishing the Temporal Power would be a
crime to be reprobated by every decent human being,
and the letting loose of a frightful scourge upon
humanity, from which even a fiend himself might recoil,
that he evidently believes it would be an act so excellent
as to command the applause of every Catholic in the
world. Far be it from me to hold the Pope responsible
for so criminal a sentiment, which I am assured on the
best authority that he would abhor; but that it should
find expression in a pamphlet published under such
auspices, and handed to me in the Vatican itself, is a
striking demonstration of the extent of the pressure to
which the Holy Father must be subjected by this new
Temptation in the Wilderness.

As the pamphlet was given to me by Monsignor
Mocenni, and as it has never been translated into English, or even into French, it may be as well to give here
a brief summary of the contents, with a few extracts
illustrating its spirit and its drift.

The author begins by declaring that the Italian
Government is in a state of open war, of irreconcilable
and daily struggle with the Supreme Pontiff, the head of
the Catholic Church. The dispute is felt, even by many
in the Liberal camp, to be a worm gnawing at the very
core of the Italian kingdom, while by the Pope it is
deplored as an obstacle to the salvation of many souls.

Who, then, is to blame for its continuance? Crispi
says that the fault is the Pope's, but Crispi has lied.
The fact is that the Italian Government will not listen
to any proposal for re-establishing the Temporal Power;
while the Pope, especially as it is now manifest that the
real object of the revolution is to destroy his spiritual
authority, cannot abdicate his claims to full sovereignty
over Rome   There are many reasons for this.   The Pope
cannot regard the present Government of Italy as the
real representatives of the Italian people.   It is a
usurpation imposed by force and maintained by violence,
which refuses to its subjects even the liberty of petition-
ing for a reconciliation with the Holy See.   He is
trustee for the whole Church.   He cannot abdicate his
rights, neither can he cease to protest.   The pamphlet
is a strenuous argumentative polemic against those
Catholics who would have the Pope accept accomplished facts, and give up crying over the spilt milk of
the Temporal Power.   The second chapter, entitled
" The Pope's Protestations," tells us that " the Pope, in
the case of any negotiations, would not endure advice
or interference.   It is certain that he will never accept
any reconciliation which does not ensure a real and
sufficient territorial sovereignty, and a guarantee of his
real and manifest independence."   Therefore, let Catholics, members of a society in which the most important
point is a spirit of discipline and perfect obedience,
beware how they suggest that he can be content with
anything less.   Books advocating reconciliation on

other terms have been placed on the Index, as befits works which openly censure the acts of the Sovereign Pontiff. In the third chapter, which treats of the necessity of the Temporal Power, we are taught that a belief in the Temporal Power is almost necessary to salvation. The argument is ingenious, and runs something like this—

"All admit that where the Vicar of Christ and all the Bishops agree to teach a doctrine which concerns the universal government of the Church, they receive the special assistance promised them by Jesus Christ. All believers, therefore, are obliged meekly to accept their teaching. The necessity of the Temporal Power is a doctrine concerning the universal government of the Church. The Pope and all the Bishops agree in teaching it. Therefore, they must have been inspired by Jesus Christ, and all the faithful must accept their teaching."

The next chapter maintains that the Temporal Power is equally necessary in the eyes of reason. The other nations would never turn to the Bishop of Rome with the same faith and devotion if he were a subject of Italy as they would if he were independent. It is admitted that the Bishops of Rome occupied a position of spiritual independence when they were subjects of the Cæsars, and worshipped in the Catacombs. But, naïvely confesses the author, we might no doubt expose the Popes to the shame and the suffering of their primitive predecessors, but we cannot secure that we should be repaid by a revival of the fervid faith and love of the early Christians. Then, again, it is urged, what is the use of a small territorial sovereignty, which would leave

the Pope exposed to pressure from his powerful neigh-
bour?   The   answer   is   certainly   not   deficient   in
audacity—

> "For the Catholics and the Popes will insist upon an arrange-
> ment which is not illusory, but which will fully guarantee the full
> and absolute independence of the Head of the Church, and if for
> that much is required, so much the worse for the interests of those
> who do not wish to restore anything ! "

In the chapter, "Why the Pope cannot remain
silent," the author makes a curious comparison between
the Papal claim to the Temporal Power, and the King of
Italy's claim to the kingdoms of Cyprus and Jerusalem.
It is, however, more substantial, and the Pope is bound
by his oath and by his responsibility to the whole
Church to keep up his protest.   The memory of thirteen millions of martyrs who died for the liberties of the
Church compels him to keep up his protest.   Besides, he
has now protested so long that he cannot afford to draw
back.   "The tremendous fact of the matter is," says the
candid author, "that the more thoughtful shudder to
think of the terrible scandal which would be spread
through the world, and the triumphant sophisms of the
impious if the Pope, after all his protests as to the necessity of the Temporal Power, were explicitly or implicitly
prepared to accept the present condition of things."   By
way of strengthening the Pope's determination not to
stultify himself, we are reminded that Cavour said,
" that in Rome the temporal authority of the Pope is so
closely united to the spiritual power that the one cannot

be separated from the other without the risk of destroying both," and that Frederick the Great wrote to Voltaire—"When the sovereignty of the Popes has fallen, then we shall have conquered. As no sovereign of Europe will recognise a Vicar of Christ who is subject to another sovereign, each of them will keep his own patriarch." Then follows the famous passage about an attack on Italy, to which I have already referred.

The sixth chapter attempts to show that the Pope has ground for hoping that his Temporal Power will come back. The argument is, in brief, that it always has done so in the past, and that it therefore must do so in the future. The Holy Ghost assists the Pope to declare it is necessary, and no one can refuse to admit it without being a rebel against the supreme authority of the Church. "This doctrine being accepted by all the Episcopate, has the evident character of the Catholic doctrine"—a curious attempt to exalt the Temporal Power into a dogma of the Church. The chapter on the bearing of the Temporal Power of the Pope to the Political Unity of Italy is vigorous and interesting. It suggests the possibility of reconciling Italian unity with the Temporal Power, by substituting for the present Italian Kingdom a Federal Union of Italian States, of which, possibly, the States of the Church might be the keystone. The present régime is bitterly declared to have ruined the country by extravagance, and overwhelmed it beneath the three plagues of debt, crime, and literary decadence. A system of ruinous misgovernment, established by bloodshed and treachery, maintained by force in the interest not so much of a party as of an anti-religious sect, is not a system to which, for the sake of Italy, the Pope should capitulate. Even with the Monarchy, however, a reconciliation might be possible, if it were not that the faction in power are dominated by a diabolical hatred of the Catholic Church, not as claimant to the temporal sovereignty of Rome, but as the representative of the Christian faith against the worship of Satan. The hope for the restoration of Pontifical sovereignty is declared to lie in the awakening common sense of the Italian people. It is even asserted that the fruit seems ripe. Imminent national bankruptcy and widespread corruption have so disgusted the Italians, that "if to-day we were to propose to the people the choice between federal and the centralised unity at present existing, at least half the nation, without distinction of political views, would vote for the former." In 1887-8, when 500,000 signatures were affixed to a petition in favour of conciliation, it was expected that 2,000,000 would have signed had the Government not interfered to prevent it. In Rome itself the real Roman citizens, voting according to the directions of the Pope, are overborne by the imported employés of the Administration. "We do not mean to pretend that amongst the Catholics themselves, especially amongst the Romans, those whose private interests the renewal of the Pontifical Government would injure would not feel the bitterness of their own losses.

Ground rents have risen, and an immense capital has been sunk in new buildings. All this would be damaged if the Temporal Power was restored. But Catholics all the world over cannot admit that the head of the Catholic Church should remain perpetually in subjection out of regard for the house owners of new Rome." Besides, even if some were ruined, there would be economic compensations; for one of the most powerful contributory causes of Italy's financial ruin is the obstinate maintenance of Papal spoliation, necessitating a costly foreign policy and ruinous armaments. The chapter on the Destiny of Rome draws a glowing picture of the glories of the Papacy. "The primitive history of modern nations consists solely in the stupendous pictures representing the increasing activity of Rome in the civilising of the world," and it is even asserted that the centuries to come will treasure among the acts of civilising usefulness the numerous Encyclicals in which the present Pope gave the right of direction to philosophical study, renewed the condemnation of the rascally Masonic sect, and warned people against the insidious teachings of Socialism. He has deserved under this last head the thanks even of heretical potentates, who are impotent to cope with this monster by main force. Rome, the destined seat of the Papacy, will always remain the city of the Pope. The exile at Avignon lasted seventy years, but the Pope returned in splendour. As it has been, so it will be, world without end, is the suggestion rather than the assertion of the

F

writer. In the chapter on the Pope as Sovereign a bold challenge is thrown down to history. " It is in the lives of the Popes that Kings and Emperors will find the finest examples of good government, and the peoples the ideal of a kingdom administered to the best advantage of its subjects." Suppose, then, the Pope were on his throne again ; how would he govern Rome ? He would be a Constitutional Monarch of the German type, really sovereign, who would not only reign but govern. He would be a Constitutional Prince, exercising real power. The real difficulty is popular indifference to representative institutions. It is difficult to get a quorum in the Chambers, and almost impossible to get the electors to the polls. No one takes an interest in the Parliamentary system. Why should the Pope attempt to establish institutions which are not even popular, and are based on the anti-social and anti-Christian conception of the sovereignty of the people ? What the Pope would do would be to give his subjects a statute analogous to, but not identical with, modern constitutions. He would grant a charter similar to those granted in the Middle Ages, which provided for the moderating of the power of the Prince by deputies not representing the supposed sovereignty of the people, but who, being nominated by the people, were associated with the Administration for the fixing of taxes and other specified classes of business. As for liberty of the press and liberty of worship, the Pope would interpret them in his own way. He would never admit principles intrinsically immoral, and he would make use of the repressive censure to check the licence which now daily insults religion and morality. "The scarecrow of a mediæval State," says our author, "thus resolves itself into smoke." Most Protestant readers will come to an exactly opposite conclusion, notwithstanding the comforting assurance at the close that "the Popes were always men of their century, and so they will be now."

The conclusion of the above pamphlet is an ingenious argument leading up to the doctrine that no Catholic can question the necessity of the Temporal Power without grievous danger of mortal sin. This is the way in which these new fetters for the conscience are forged. "What," asks the author, "is the counsel that every Catholic ought to follow with regard to the acts of the Vicar of Jesus Christ in governing the Church? A glance around suffices to show that the whole Catholic Episcopate and the faithful follow but one rule—viz, to conform their judgment and sentiments to those of the Supreme Pontiff, and to help him in all things, allowing ourselves with docility to be guided by him. Notwithstanding this universal rule, there are some Catholics who believe that they are permitted to judge in their hearts and even in public the acts of the Pope, to set themselves against him, and even to try and influence public opinion against his words and his acts." It is against these the author of the pamphlet directs his heaviest artillery. These recalcitrant Catholics, it seems, accuse the Vatican party of extending the dogma of Infallibility, so as to cover the political acts of the Pope. Our author begins by admitting that all Catholics believe that politically the head of the Church can commit mistakes, and then puts his best foot foremost to prove that this doctrine of the Temporal Power does so intimately concern the spiritual interests of the Church as almost to become a necessary corollary of the dogma in question. The Pope, even if he were not infallible, is not to be criticised. A father is not infallible in his family, nor the general in the army; nevertheless, no son, or soldier, or official has the right to pronounce judgment on the acts of his superior either in the army or in the family. The suppression of criticism on the Pope's demands for the Temporal Power is not because such criticism is sacrilege or heresy, but as insubordination and sedition. The acts of the sovereign are always withdrawn from public discussion and censure. Liberty of discussion is limited even in the civil state, by denying it to soldiers, who must obey the orders of their commanders; it would be intolerable to extend it without limits to the Church which Christ constituted on principles which were anything but those of modern democracy. In the Church the people cannot even imagine themselves sovereign; they are subject to the authority of the Pope, to whom they must submit, as to the Vicar of Jesus Christ. Even when Catholics are democrats as citizens, they are monarchists as Catholics. In ordinary times, all that is required of them is that they should allow themselves to be led and taught; in stormy times, like the present, we have every reason to believe that the Holy Ghost wishes to help with special lights him into whose hands He has placed the government of the Church. This ought to extinguish in any ordinary believer any desire to condemn the acts of Christ's Vicar as inopportune or erroneous. But much less should suffice to stop the gabble of any one who was tempted to make himself a public censor of the acts of the Holy See. Advice may be given secretly and submissively without objection; but to publish criticisms of his action in the press is to repudiate the direction of the Pope, and to be guilty of a seditious attempt to turn the faithful from the obedience that they owe to the great Shepherd. Their writings are dictated by a spirit of evident insubordination; from being sheep they set themselves up as ardent judges; therefore, let them be silent, at the peril of being censured by the Church and rejected by the Catholic masses with just disdain. Such is the substance of the pamphlet which Monsignor Mocenni gave me as an authoritative exposition of the views of the Vatican. Outside the Vatican, among the intelligent Catholics, I found a very different sentiment existing. The following observation was made to me by a devoted Catholic, who holds a position in the Vatican, but who has eyes to see the actual facts of the world outside:—

"If the Italian Government cared to make a great enemy, it could do so to-morrow, by simply handing over to the Pope the sovereignty of the city of Rome. Leo the Thirteenth would find himself hopelessly at a loss to discharge the duties of the position for which he sighs. None of the indispensable instruments of government are ready to his hand. He has neither employés, financiers, police, soldiers, nor any other administrative officials. In less than a week the bad elements that lurk in every great city would have made a revolution, and in a fortnight the Italian troops would be enthusiastically welcomed as the only force by which Rome could be rescued from anarchy and bloodshed."

It is obvious enough to those who are sufficiently outside to be able to watch the struggle between the opposing forces that if the Pope were to succumb, and were to use his influence to incite France to make war on Italy, and if that war resulted in the most signal success for French arms, no man would ever be more bitterly cursed with the burden of a granted prayer than Leo XIII. would be on the day when his Temporal Sovereignty was re-established in Rome by the bayonets of the French soldiery. Between him and the Italian people would be a vast gulf, filled with the blood of brave men butchered to put him back; and he would begin to reign in Rome amid the execrations of a population, every other householder of which would have been ruined by the ejection of the Italian Government from the city. When Victor Emmanuel took over the government of Rome from Pio Nono, there were only 215,000 persons in the city. To-day there are more than 400,000. The population, therefore, has doubled since Rome became the capital, and if it ceased to be the capital, one-half of the population would find themselves in the air. Catholics and Liberals alike agree that even now if the Pope were to be installed in the Quirinal in the plenitude of his ancient sovereignty, he could not hold Rome three days without a foreign garrison. What

chance would there be when between him and his subjects there was the bitter blood feud of a war, in which
France had conquered Italy for the sake of the Pope?
The Pope, then, would have to rely upon a foreign garrison, if he were not to see his priests assassinated in the
streets. Of two things one: (1) Either that garrison
would be absolutely at his orders, in which case the
Pope would govern Rome by coercion in such a fashion
as would of necessity arouse against him and his Church
the liveliest detestation of every Liberal in England, Ireland, and America; or (2) the French Republic, which
furnished the garrison, would insist on the recognition of
certain fundamental modern liberties in the government
of the Papal States. In that event the last case of the
Pope would be worse than the first. He would be but
the bailiff of the French Republic, governing a hostile
population which hated him, on principles dictated to
him by the representatives of the French Revolution.

"He needs a long spoon who would sup with the
de'il," and the Pope is no exception to the universal
rule. Even the shadow of a possible war for the re-
covery of the Temporal Power darkens the hearts of men,
and distracts the attention of the Sovereign Pontiff from
the consideration of his more strictly spiritual functions.

If the Pope is to fulfil his greater ideal, he will have
to shake himself free from the influences of the Vatican.
The atmosphere of the place, the traditions and associations which cling to its very walls, and the all-pervading
presence of the Italian Cardinals and great officials

render it impossible for him to rise to the height of his great conception of his rôle as the mouthpiece of the conscience of universal Christendom, which speaks with the voice of God.   Until he has definitely rid himself of the desire to re-establish a temporal authority in a second-rate European city, that minor and earthly ambition will continually obscure his higher and brighter ideal, and lead him into devious courses, which will impair his influence even in the Catholic world.   The Temporal Power has got on to the nerves of the Church, and it has come to be to many in the Vatican the only thing worth living for.   So far from sharing that view, it seems to me that the re-establishment of the Temporal Power would be the greatest curse that could be inflicted upon the Church.   And after my visit to Rome, I realise more vividly than before how much justification there was for the prophecy with which some months before I concluded my paper in the *Contemporary Review*.   " It may be that the Church of Rome has played her part in the affairs of men, and that in the new English-speaking era, on the threshold of which mankind is standing, there may be no more than a niche in a Roman museum for the successor of Hildebrand.   In that case, whether the Pope stays in Rome or goes to Seville or Innsbruck or Minorca does not much matter.   But if there be any real substance of truth in the Pope's belief that the Catholic Church is the chosen instrument whereby Infinite Wisdom, inspired by Eternal Love, works out the salvation of the world, then as certainly as it was necessary for the persecution to arise to scatter the first Christians from Jerusalem, so that they might carry the seed of the faith over the Roman world, not less certainly shall we see in a few years, or even it may be a few months, the breaking of a storm which will compel the Pope to fly from the Eternal City—never to return. And in that hour when those who hate the Church fill the air with insult and exultation, and when those who love her more in her accidents than in her essence are abased to the dust with humiliation and shame, then to the eye of faith the enforced hegira of the Pope from the Latin to the English world will be regarded as the supreme affirmation of the providential mission of the Church—a new divine commission for her to undertake on a wider basis the great task of rebuilding the City of God."

· CHAPTER VI.

THE GOOD WORK OF THE CHURCH.

EVERYTHING that in Rome is interesting is chiefly interesting because it takes the mind away from Rome.
That which is visible is important as a finger-post for the
invisible. Everything that you see is, as it were, an eye-
hole through which you look into an infinite beyond.
Usually that infinitude is of the past. A mouldering
stone recalls the glories of the Cæsars; a crumbling battle-
ment the horrors of siege and sack; an unnamed grave
the sacrifices of the innumerable saints by whose deaths
we live. But it is not only of the past that the elo-
quence of the very stones of Rome is great, in proportion
as it silences the arid dispute between the Vatican and
the Quirinal, that fills the air as with the croaking of bull-
frogs in the marsh, and compels men to hear the distant
voices which, in realms that Cæsar never knew, are
sounding in the ears of men. From the point of view of
the past, it is difficult to say which is the most sacred
place in Rome. But from the point of view of the
living present, there can be no doubt at all. It is not to

be found in the Vatican or St. Peter's, much less is it to
be found in the king's palace at the Quirinal. The most
sacred place, where life is most centred, is the plain and
unpretending College of the Propaganda, in the Piazza
di Spagna. Baedeker dismisses it in six lines and a
half, and nine-tenths of the tourists never notice its
existence. But it is from that dingy building, now half-
concealed by scaffolding, and chiefly noted as standing
in the shadow of the column from the summit of which
Mary, standing in the crescent moon, and with the stars
of heaven around her head, looks down upon the square,
that the great heart beats whose pulsations are felt to
the uttermost ends of the world. It is in the midst of
the king's city. On either side rattle over the roughly-
paved streets the noisy little omnibuses that ply in Rome.
Behind it rises the far more pretentious newspaper office
which has just been built for the *Popolo Romano*. Close
to it, in the Via de' Due Macelli, a gleaming electric
light advertises the existence of a café chantant. Yet
there, as much in the midst of the world, the flesh, and
the devil as it would be in any heathen land, the great
Missionary Society of Rome stands to-day.

It is nothing to look at outside, and inside its chief
characteristic is want of room. It is a large building,
but it is all too small for its purposes. Everything is
cramped for space. All is for work, nothing is for show.
But I never passed that stuccoed front without a homage,
which I never paid to the relics of the saints. For out
from that plain edifice have gone for nearly three

hundred years the apostles who carry into every land
the sacred flame of Christian faith. The other week,
early in the morning, seventeen students were consecrated in the church which stands in the centre of the
building, who after their departure might never meet
again on earth. East and west, and north and south, as
far as the foot of man can tread, fare forth these devoted
legionaries of the Church, bent upon the subduing of all
nations, and on the establishment of the universal
kingdom of our Lord and His Christ.

It was my good fortune to be taken over the college
by Monsignor Jacobini—not yet Cardinal Jacobini.
There was a Cardinal Jacobini some years ago, who
filled Cardinal Rampolla's place as Papal Secretary
of State, and there will be a Cardinal Jacobini again,
and it will be well for the Church if he should be
spared to occupy even a higher office than his name-
sake. For of all the men whom I have met in Rome,
Monsignor Jacobini impresses me the most favourably.
He was born an Italian, it is true, which is one of the
misfortunes for which he can hardly be held account-
able. He is young, being not much over fifty, and in
the full prime of life. For eight years now he has been
Secretary of the Propaganda—that is to say, he has held
a post corresponding to that of secretary of all our Protestant missionary societies put together. Over him is
Cardinal Simeoni, a grave, earnest, and laborious prelate, who toils at his post as an English judge of the old
school does at the bench. He is Prefect of the Propa-

ganda, the Pope's *alter ego* in all that concerns the missionary side of the Church. After him Monsignor Jacobini is the most important pivot of the Congregation. He is not tall—good stuff in him, as so often happens, being made up in a small bundle. But his well-knit frame is almost incapable of exhaustion; his mind is quick and sympathetic, and there is a kindly humour in his eye which endears him to all who know him. The only woe that he has to dread is that pronounced upon those of whom all men speak well. Black or red, Catholic or Free Thinker, all men praise Monsignor Jacobini. During the day he toils at his desk as the galley-slave toils at his oar, and in the evening he takes his recreation in looking after the interests of an Artist's and Workman's Catholic Association, of which he and a well-known Roman Count are the leading supporters. This society is partly for mutual help in case of illness or want of employment, partly for recreation, and partly for education. It contains about 3,000 members, and is one of the most excellent of the institutions of Rome. Of all the hopeful signs for the future of the Church, and for its utilisation as an instrument of social amelioration, one of the most hopeful is the fact that Monsignor Jacobini is where he is, close to the heart of the Church militant, and the intimate friend and confidential adviser of the Pope.

Our Protestant missionary societies are hardly a hundred years old. The Congregation of the Propaganda was founded in 1622 by Gregory XV., and has been work-

ing ever since. On the shelves of the College are archives
recording an activity that has never ceased, and which it
is devoutly to be hoped will never cease. Great volumes
of letters, bound in parchment, stand side by side, bearing eloquent but silent witness to the self-denying
labours of hundreds of thousands of devoted men and
women who have gone forth to labour and to die *in
partibus infidelium.* Their handwriting is faint and
faded now, but with how fiery a zeal were the pens
guided which traced these characters! What innumerable
dramas, full of the noblest human heroism, enacted not
in full amphitheatre before an applauding or even a
hostile throng, but lived out day by day in obscurity, in
disease, in neglect, without hope of praise or of earthly
reward! They wrote their epistles with their blood, and
sealed their testimony with their lives. Men of the
highest education, and women of the most refined tastes
and of the gentlest birth, sent to labour among the black
fellows of Australia or the Hottentots of Africa, if by
any means they might save some, have left their only
written record here—in these few fragmentary records
of their difficulties. Their real record is to be found,
not here, but in the lives of their converts, in the tribes
reclaimed from savagery, in the families which they have
humanised, in the children whom they have educated, in
the women whom they have raised from being the
chattels of brutes into some semblance of the mother
of Christ. As I walked round the crowded shelves
in the archives of the Propaganda, and thought of all that

vast mass of unknown valour, of love stronger than death, and of services to the lapsed and the lost, I grudged the old saints their monopoly of the altar-pieces, and would willingly have sacrificed a whole hecatomb of St. Sebastians for a few tributes to these St. Sebastians and St. Cecilias of our own time.

The Museum of the Propaganda is interesting enough, but for lack of space it is impossible to display its treasures. They do not keep the portraits of the missionaries, they have not even the portraits of their martyrs. There is an invaluable collection of ancient codices, rare and curious MSS., a collection which is the product of the industry of the emissaries of the College in every part of the world. There is a collection of 23,000 coins of all degrees of value heaped up in chests as so much bullion. Here, also, is the famous map of the world on which Pope Alexander VI., in olden times, drew the dividing line, allocating one half of the western hemisphere to Portugal and the other half to Spain. The great chart-occupies the central position in the large room, flanked by trophies of arms collected from the troops of the Mahdi, and idols from the Farther East. It is an interesting memorial of the rôle played by the Popes in the old days, of the intrepidity with which they acted upon such scanty information as they possessed, and of their utter inability to foresee or to control events. On the northern continent thus summarily parcelled out, all on this side to Spain, all on that side to Portugal, not one rood remains in possession of either Power to-day. The whole has passed into the ownership of English - speaking men. Another curiosity of the Museum is the original map of Marco Polo, which Monsignor Jacobini recently sent to London for exhibition. In those days Rome was the storehouse of the knowledge of the world, a kind of British Association for the advancement of science in germ. The collections of birds and insects are much crowded, and are interesting chiefly because of the attention which they show to have been paid by the Catholic missionaries to the natural history of the countries in which they lived. If our missionary societies are wise, they will establish *en permanence* a missionary museum on a large scale in London, and before doing so, they had better send a delegate to Monsignor Jacobini to inspect the collection at the Propaganda.

In an obscure corner of the Museum, behind a gigantic elephant tusk, lies the jewelled cross of an Italian order bestowed by the Italian kingdom on the late Cardinal Massaia, in recognition of his services to humanity and civilisation in Abyssinia and Ethiopia. The Cardinal refused the decoration. "How can I receive this jewelled star," he asked, "from the hands of the men who have plundered the Propaganda?" For the Italian kingdom has laid violent hands upon the property accumulated for the diffusion of the faith among the heathen, giving the Propaganda Italian stock in exchange for the confiscated estates. So

Cardinal Massaia refused the order, and it lies to-day in the Museum, a silent but eloquent witness at once to the sterling merit which wrung such a tribute from the enemy, and to the bitterness of feeling engendered by the feud between the Pope and the King.

From the Museum we passed through the various offices where the business of the Propaganda is performed. Under the Propaganda are all the English-speaking countries. Russia is specially taken under the care of the Vatican, and its affairs are not under Cardinal Simeoni. But England, Ireland, Scotland, America, and the Colonies are all *in partibus infidelium*. So, in fact, are all the best parts of the world. The work is divided into two portions, the East and the West. All those of the Óriental robe are under the charge of Monsignor Persico. When I visited the College he was at Constantinople, and I did obeisance to his empty room, in recognition of the hardship to which he was subjected in having his name associated with the Persico "Rescript," the issue of which was quite one of the worst blunders of the present reign. Down the corridor on the opposite side to Monsignor Persico's room are the offices of the Minutante, or précis writers, as we should say. Everywhere there was too little accommodation. The affairs of Greece and those of the United States of America have only one office between them. I looked with natural curiosity at the room where sit the permanent officials charged with the control of the department of Great Britain and Ireland.

G

As usual, they are Italians. In the whole Propaganda there is not one Englishman or American. There is one antediluvian Irishman, who is connected in some way with the Congregation; but it is forty years and more since he visited his native land, and the very stones which surround the dead heart of O'Connell in the church of St. Agatha have more sympathy with the Irish movement to-day than has my old travelling companion, the solitary old Irish Benedictine, who alone of English-speaking men has the right officially to visit the Propaganda. Monsignor Jacobini, with his natural insight into the core of things, is working hard at English. He spends about three hours a day with an English priest, who acts as English tutor.

After visiting the Hall of the Congregation, where, as we should say, the committee of management holds its meeting, under the presidency of Cardinal Simeoni—the average attendance is about twelve—and where the papers nominating all the English, Irish, and American bishops are signed, we went in succession through the College and the church, and then visited the printing-office of the Propaganda. It is about to flit across the way to new premises, where it will have more elbow-room. At present it is almost as much too small for the demand upon its cases as a certain printing-office which shall be nameless, not a hundred miles from Charing Cross. One room was set apart for producing in very handsome style the new edition of the works of St. Thomas Aquinas, who is at present in the highest favour with the Pope. Here are printed all the publications of the Propaganda. They cast their own type, bind their own books, and do almost everything except make their own paper. The "comps." at the Propaganda set type in as many languages as those who are employed for our Bible Society. As a sample of their resources, they have produced the Lord's Prayer in 250 different languages, in 180 different characters. Necessarily, the Propaganda is one of the most polyglot places in the world. Jerusalem on the day of Pentecost was nothing to the College in the Piazza di Spagna. There are 120 students resident in the College, and some 300 more attend the lectures. Between them they are said to speak seventy different languages. When Monsignor Jacobini gives a reception, you begin to realise something of the mischief that was done by the confusion of tongues. It is about time that English began to supersede all other tongues as the common language of the world. Although they talk all languages, official correspondence is carried on only in three—namely, French, Latin, and German. On an average, about 50 letters are received and answered daily, and the office boy, who has the run of the waste-paper basket, ought to possess one of the finest collections of foreign postage stamps extant.

From the printing-house we visited the new premises in the Piazza di Spagna, which, as soon as the French pilgrims are out of the way, will be occupied in the basement by the printers, and upstairs by the professors.

The building, when I visited it, was filled—even the picture gallery — with improvised beds for the French pilgrims, whose presence in Rome is one of the most notable features of the present situation. The class-rooms are large and airy, and the students are much to be congratulated upon their approaching change of quarters.

I left the Propaganda with the conviction that, so far as vast portions of the world are concerned, the Catholic Church is an enormous, an incalculable power for good. Whatever men may think about their doctrines as to the life beyond the grave, the men who have gone out from this College, and who are directed and controlled by the Congregation of the Propaganda, are an effective, moral, and civilising force of the first value in all that concerns the social and material amelioration of the lot of uncivi-lised man.   There are hundreds of millions of human beings who are as much in need of the civilising word as were our ancestors when Gregory heralded by a pious pun the conversion of the English world.   The Catholic missionaries may not make the most of their oppor-tunities.   Few of us do.   They may devote too much time in preparing a bridge over which the soul can pass into paradise, and spend too little in remedying the evils which convert so much of this life into a hell.   But, take them with all their limitations and shortcomings, who can deny that at least for all the savages of the world here is an effective instrument, for the existence of which mankind has cause to be grateful?   On all the three

points concerning which I came to inquire, the Church
in these regions and among uncivilised man has no
reason to fear inquiry. It is true that its missionaries,
especially in the East, are French rather than English,
and would, if they could, make the world Latin rather
than Anglo-Saxon. They can no more do it than the
Pope could secure that North America should be
divided between Spain and Portugal. All that they do
comes ultimately to our net. Catholic missionaries,
Jesuits or men of the Propaganda, preceded us in
America, and in India they were but the foreign van-
guard of the English advance. They sow, we reap. Nor
will the influence of tradition long permit the Catholic
missionaries to look to France rather than to England as
their natural protector. The very archives of the Propaganda bear witness in their mutilation to the rude
violence with which the French, under the first
Napoleon, ransacked the treasures of the Church. The
Republic which compels the religious orders to seek
refuge on English soil cannot long command the
enthusiasm of Catholic missionaries even in the Farther
East.

From the point of view of the Socialist, the missionary
activity of the Church is pure gain. To the vague aspirations of the semi-savage man for a more human life,
these teachers return a prompt and effective response.
Not less, and sometimes more than the missionaries of
other creeds, they are the devoted Servants of Man. If
the Church could do for the modern civilised world what

the poorest of the missionary orders do for the tribes among whom they labour, we should not in Italy and in France to-day be living *in partibus infidelium.* All that the early Church did for the barbarians of Europe, the Church to-day is doing for the barbarians of Asia, of Africa, and of Polynesia. To teach letters, to inculcate industry, to war against war, to suppress the slave trade, to diffuse the arts, to introduce all that differentiates man from beast—these are social services to be welcomed with gratitude and enthusiasm, even if those who render this service are vowed to obedience to the Pope of Rome or to the General of the Society of Jesus.

Nor is this less the case in relation to the third great group of questions that concern the position of woman. On the lower plane of savage and semi-civilised, and, in fact, of all but the most advanced civilisation of Christendom, even the lowest Catholic ideal represents an enormous advance. Woman outside Christendom, with few exceptions, is not an individual, much less a soul. She is a chattel, to be used or abused at the will of her owner. Nothing but good can follow the apparition of such sweet and saintly Sisters as those whom I saw in the anteroom of Monsignor Jacobini, in the midst of populations whose only idea of woman is that of a two-legged beast of burden, whom it is an amusement to degrade. The most reactionary Catholic is at least a monogamist, and monogamy represents an ideal to which one-half of the human race has not yet attained. After all, the first step which counts, and which logically includes everything, is gained when men learn that a woman has a soul as valuable as their own. So far, therefore, all is plain sailing. The real problem only arises when we come to consider the relations between the Church and the modern world.

CHAPTER VII.

THE CHURCH AND THE MODERN WORLD.

THAT the Church, tested by the three conditions laid down in these letters, is doing a good and useful work among races of inferior civilisation is indisputable. She is still the apostle of culture, the teacher of letters, the pioneer of colonisation, the improver of agriculture, the mother of arts and letters. This glory she shares with all the Christian Churches; but the most hostile Protestant admits her supremacy in the mission-field, even although he qualifies his admission by asserting that she is but *prima inter pares*. But we find a very different state of things when we turn from the civilising activity of the apostles of the Propaganda among races of heathen creed and inferior civilisation to the complex and highly-developed society of modern Christendom. Here even the most devoted Catholic will regretfully admit the Church can no longer even pretend to be the leader of the onward march of Humanity. He may put it down to the devil, or to the exceeding wickedness of a perverse and rebellious generation; but, however he may explain it, the fact is patent and indisputable.

Mazzini roundly declared that not a single one of the vast strides made upon the path of progress in our age was either suggested or consecrated by the Catholic Church, and he irreverently compared the hierarchy that met at the Vatican to proclaim the doctrine of Infallibility to "motionless sphinxes in the vast desert, who inertly contemplate the shadow of the centuries as they pass, while Humanity, whom they should have guided, has gone otherwhere." All this I may say without offence, for there is no one who sees it more vividly and laments it more keenly than the best Catholics in Europe, who are anything but motionless sphinxes. Whatever may be their mistakes, there is no doubt that the Comte de Mun in France, Herr Windthorst in Germany, Cardinal Manning in England, Archbishops Walsh and Croke in Ireland, Cardinal Gibbons in America, Cardinal Moran in Australia, and Monsignor Jacobini and the Pope himself in Italy, all are labouring honestly at the very uphill task of regaining for the Church somewhat of its former position in Christendom. They know they have lost it, and nowhere more utterly than in the Latin countries, where they once held undisputed sway. Whether they can regain it is a problem about which they are sanguine in proportion to the faith that is in them; and the more they believe, the more they will welcome every honest criticism which, perhaps, may here or there afford them a hint or a suggestion that they may, from their superior knowledge, be able to turn to good account.

It is therefore without fear of giving offence that I
must put on record my conviction that, so far as I can
see, the Vatican, as at present constituted and controlled, is about as fit to undertake profitably the
guidance of the social revolution of Christendom as the
ruins of the Forum—after the Forum, the Vatican is
almost the most archaic ruin in Rome—are competent
to undertake the federation of the British Empire.
When I speak of the resemblance between the great
central points of the two systems of Imperial and Papal
Rome, I speak solely from the point of view of the
secular side of human life, and nothing that I say refers
at all to the theological side of the Church. The Forum
is a visible, unmistakable ruin. Here and there a stately
pillar towers aloft, unbroken by the weight of two
thousand years; but it is an exception. Temples and
palaces and courts are now to be traced but by their
foundations. Antiquarian zeal has unearthed much of
the ancient pavement, on which the Roman cats sun
themselves in the early morning close to the rostrum
from which Cicero pleaded—the sole occupants of a
tribunal whose decrees were once potent from the
Ultima Thule of the northern seas to the remotest East.
The colossal ruins of the Flavian Amphitheatre—the
St. Peter's of the Pagan world,—the triumphal arches of
Constantine and of Titus, the Capitol, once the supreme
goal that crowned the Roman triumph, now a mere
museum of precious fragments snatched from the wrecks
of time, all attest, in a fashion too plain to be misunder-

stood, that the Forum, once the nerve-centre of the world, from which all roads ran, and where was woven into one mighty whole the great web of Roman laws, is now only the monumental sepulchre of a dead Empire.

Yet the forces which surged from that Roman heart are far from being spent. Roman law, Roman ideals, and Roman customs mould the life of those who boast themselves of being the heirs of all the ages. There is not a single lumberman in the forests of the North-West, nor a digger in the mines of Australia, but in his inmost heart and soul bears the ineffaceable stamp of those stern men of iron mould who, in ancient time, made this wilderness of ruin the proud temple of universal law. Desolate and dead as it is to-day, it was once the living womb of our civilisation. Life which went out from here has vitalised the world. It has multiplied itself from a thousand centres, and goes on multiplying with unabated force. But in the Forum itself life is not. No hurrying feet now tread the uneven blocks which mark the pavement of the Via Sacra; no car now climbs in triumph to the Capitol. All is still—silent as the crater of some extinct volcano whose fiery lava had once overwhelmed a world. As you listen and remember, you hear a far-off murmur of many sounds; the hum of the busy mart; the roar of applauding crowds; the sharp clash of arms, all mingling indistinct and distant like the subdued sound of the sea-surge within the convolutions of the shell. And as it is with the Forum, so, in relation to the social and political activities of the

world, it has come to be with the Vatican. From it
also has ebbed, and is still ebbing, the great tide of
human life. From it there went forth a great word that
has done much to the civilised world. The influences
which it diffused are living and active to-day in every
centre of human life. Its churches, with fissiparous
vitality, increase and multiply in realms of which St. Peter
never heard, and its missionaries carry the cross over
seas the vast expanse of which would have affrighted
the simple fishermen of Galilee. But although the
Roman faith lives on imperishable in the hearts and
lives of men, strong in the strength of innumerable
sainted lives, and energised by the electric force of a
myriad martyrdoms, the life is in the extremities rather
than in the centre. The Vatican is, of course, not
stranded so high above the ocean level of the life of to-
day as is the Forum. The halberdiers still pace to and fro
in the vestibule; the Papal chamberlains are in attendance in the antechamber; and still to Rome at stated
periods come pilgrims and prelates paying homage. It
is still the centre of a great Church, the capital of a
religion which overspreads the world. But—regarded
as an institution fitted to direct, and guide, and control
the secular forces of the modern world, as the early
Popes directed and guided the forces of their time—the
Vatican is almost as archaic as the Forum. The Holy
See, no doubt, has an immense past; but if it is to have
a great future, it will have to readjust its machinery to
the times. The Pope declares that the Church must

address itself to the social question. But, unless the more intelligent and progressive party is able to remodel, or at least to develop, the existing Church, we might almost as well go to the Forum for help in passing Home Rule as go to the Vatican for assistance in the social legislation of the future.

It is not that the Pope and his advisers do not wish well to good causes; and, so far as they can, they would like to lend a helping hand to anything that would really tend in their opinion to ameliorate the lot of the people. But they are not linked on in any real vital fashion to the organic life of the world. Their priests, no doubt, are constantly brought into contact with the individual facts which, taken together, make up the sum of life. But the collective troubles of the race or of the nation—the problems with which philanthropists have to deal, and for which Parliaments have to legislate—do not, in the ordinary course of the Pope's business, come officially before the Holy See at all. It is no part of any one's business to keep the Pope informed upon the questions upon which at any moment he may be asked to pronounce an opinion. He has his solemn apparatus of masses and prayers duly provided for to keep him in due orthodox relation with his Father who is in Heaven; he is almost totally unprovided with even the most elementary arrangement for keeping him in touch with the actual necessities of his brothers, who are scattered over all the surface of the earth. Hence at present, and until the better men who are in sympathy with modern ideas are able to expel the evil old spirit which cripples and confines the scope of the action of the Holy See to a purely spiritual world, the utmost that social reformers can hope for the Pope is that he will content himself with emitting pious opinions in favour of an amelioration of the conditions of labour in the abstract, and that he will scrupulously abstain from intermeddling any further in matters which he has neither the training to understand, the advisers to correct his ignorance, nor the information necessary to enable him to pronounce an intelligent judgment.   I do not say that if we had a vigorous young Pope, with enough iron in his blood to enable him to readjust the Holy See to the altered necessities of the new time, we might not find in the chair of St. Peter some one competent to play the great part of international director-in-chief of the humanitarian forces of the world.   But before that could be effected, a great deal will have to be changed.

"Yes, I should think so," sneers a pessimist sceptic at my elbow.   "About as much as would be necessary to convert the Via Sacra in the Forum into a modern railway junction."   I do not think so.   I may be utterly wrong, but it seems to me that the signs are hopeful that the Papacy may be led irresistibly into the road which would give the Holy See once more its old position at the head of the world, and of those signs by far the most hopeful is the destruction of the Temporal Power.   That power, no doubt, had its uses, other-

wise it would not have been permitted. But its uses
have been exhausted, and it has disappeared, and in the
interest of the Church I hope it has disappeared for
ever. As a man never learns to swim so long as he
dares not trust himself to the support of the water, so the
Popes will not realise what their influence in the world
might be until they cease to cling anxiously with one foot
to the rock of temporal authority. This is the pre-
requisite of any real exercise of Papal influence in
the social sphere, if only because it would, for the
first time, give them time to think about the great
problems of our age at present. For one thought
that is spared in the Vatican to the amelioration of the
condition of mankind, there must be a hundred devoted
to the restoration of the Temporal Power.

When I first went to the Vatican, prepared to hail
with eager welcome every indication, however faint, that
at the headquarters of the Church there was something
of the same spirit that prevails in the Archiepiscopal
Palaces of Westminster and Dublin, I was somewhat
rudely disabused of my illusion. In the office of the
Secretary of State, the high official who received me
seemed to think of nothing so much as the Temporal
Power. That was the *sine quâ non.* That was the first
indispensable. There even seemed some courteous surprise that any one could deem the questions which I had
come to urge as even worth consideration, compared with
the all-important, all-engrossing subject of the restoration
of the Temporal Sovereignty of the Pope. It was as if a

man had travelled from afar to learn from the lips of some great physician how a terrible pestilence might be stayed, and the only counsel which he heard was, "To offer a cock to Esculapius." Nay, it was worse; for after the cock had been offered no one would have been one penny the worse, whereas, if the Temporal Power were re-established, the difficulty of utilising the Church for humanitarian purposes would have been immeasurably increased.

Of course, I am aware that the attitude, which, I admit, is by no means universal, can easily be explained. The Pope, who never makes a speech without sighing over his altered fortunes, is nearly eighty. He is an Italian, born and bred in the conviction that the Pope must reign as king in Rome. An old Jacobite could no more forsake the Stuarts than Leo XIII. could abandon his dream. That is no doubt true. But it does not help us much to get the work done which the dream retards. There is a characteristic story told of Herbert Bismarck, which supplies a fitting answer to those who allege the age and inveterate prejudice of the Pope as if to account for a misfortune were the same thing as to justify it. When the German Emperor arrived in Rome, the Chamberlain of the King attempted to enter the railway carriage to welcome the young Kaiser. He was rudely jostled by Count Herbert, who thrust the Chamberlain back, exclaiming, "Out of the way. I am Count Bismarck." The Chamberlain stepped back, and remarked quietly to the insolent German, "The explanation is ample, but the excuse is insufficient."

So it may be said of the Vatican. Early training, great age, and inveterate prejudice afford an ample explanation as to why so many at headquarters persist in playing the rôle of Bunyan's Man with the Muck Rake; but as an excuse for a pre-occupation so prejudicial to the real work that waits to be done, it is certainly inadequate.

There is a story told of the visit of some delegates from Palestine on a mission to Caligula, which somewhat aptly illustrates the impression certain to be produced on all who go to Rome at present in search of light and guidance on the social and political problems of our time. The Empire was then in its early splendour. Its representatives ruled with absolute authority over the whole civilised world. Humanity rejoiced under the great boon of the Roman peace, and the august mortal who swayed the sceptre of the world was regarded as almost divine. To the eyes of the outer world nothing could be more imposing or more manifestly providential than the great fabric of the Roman Empire. But as the ambassadors of Israel came within, and sought to execute their mission by a personal audience with the Emperor, they experienced a notable disenchantment. To them it was a matter of life and death. To him it was but a troublesome trifle, for the consideration of which he grudged to spare a moment dedicated to the Imperial pleasures. For a long time they could not find him. At last, when they succeeded in gaining access to his sacred person, he put them off with frivolities, asked them why they did not eat pork,

I

and abruptly left them in the midst of the audience. Yet that buffoon and monster was the pivot round which the Roman State revolved. There is, of course, nothing at the Vatican even remotely resembling the scenes that disgraced the palaces of the Cæsars. But although the cause of the pre-occupation is different, the net result is much the same. The human pivot on which the whole Roman machine revolves, although a saint instead of a Cæsar, is still human. Extreme age, frequent infirmities, together with spiritual pr-eoccupations and a longing for temporal power, incapacitate the Pope from sparing time and energy to the consideration of the new problems which are ever emerging in the modern world.

Even the regular audiences which form part of the ordinary day's work of the Vatican have from time to time to be abandoned. The Pope has barely the strength necessary to enable him to adequately fulfil even the comparatively minor rôle which he understands and attempts to realise. The wider rôle, until we have a younger Pope and a reconstituted Curia, is utterly out of the question. At present the real control of the Holy See must remain largely in the hands of an *entourage* of permanent officials, with whom, as with any men in such a position, there is a constant temptation to postpone all subjects that are not absolutely in the day's work, and with regard to all else to fall back on the saying of Louis XV., *Après nous le déluge.* But this is not of the essence of the Papal system. It is rather a natural shortcoming, which may be rectified.

CHAPTER VIII.

AT THE RECEPTION OF THE FRENCH PILGRIMS.

ROME, Oct. 26th, 1889.

I HAVE just returned from the Vatican, where, in the Hall of Canonisation, I have attended mass said by the Pope in the presence of the pilgrims of France. These French pilgrimages, the third of which is taking place this year, are among the most notable ecclesiastico-political events of our time. Over one thousand Frenchmen, collected from all the dioceses of France, have arrived by special trains at Rome, for the purpose of assuring the Pope of their unalterable affection and devotion. They were received yesterday at the Vatican in a solemn audience, at which, thanks to the kind inter-vention of Monsignor Jacobini, of the Propaganda, I was privileged to be present in the novel capacity of a French son of labour. To-day the Pope celebrated mass, to the great delight of the faithful, not in St. Peter's, as he would have done in olden times when the Pope was master in Rome, but in the gorgeous hall in which, under the outspread wings of angels in white and gold, there is proclaimed the canonisation of those

whom, all the efforts of the *avocato del diavolo* notwithstanding, the supreme authority of the Church decrees
to be on the saints' "eternal bederoll worthy to
be fyled." All day for five days before and after Sunday
these French pilgrims are making the round of the holy
sites, filling the air with their pious canticles, saying
their prayers in the sacred sites, and indulging in the
prolonged ecstasy of a great spiritual exercise. It was a
great piece of good fortune which enabled me to witness
these high functions; and I hasten, while the impression
is still fresh upon my mind, to set down for the benefit
of those at home some account of what I have just seen
and heard.

The situation here is profoundly interesting. Every
one feels that the two opposing parties are coming at
last to death grips. Signor Crispi's speech the other
day at Palermo is but one among many signs that the
bitter feud between the Italian Government and the
Pope is so far from being appeased, that at any moment
events may precipitate a violent and, it may be, a tragic
solution of the great controversy. "Long live the Pope-
King!" "Long live the Pope-King!" was the cry which
burst from the crowded and enthusiastic company which
yesterday fell on their knees before Leo XIII., as,
preceded by his great ostrich feather fans, and borne on
the shoulders of his attendants, he slowly made his way
to the improvised throne from which he addressed a
discourse to the workmen of France. But outside the
doors of the Vatican, directing our carriages this way

and that with the autocratic authority of a London policeman, were the gendarmes of Italy; while close to the gates of the Pope's palace lay, ready to be called to arms at a moment's notice, the Italian garrison, which could be relied upon to blow the Pope and all his Cardinals as high as the dome of St. Peter's, if ever the Republic, whose sons yesterday acclaimed the Pope-King, were to make the least attempt to re-establish the temporal authority of Leo XIII. over the capital of united Italy. Seldom have I seen so much alkali in solution so close to so much acid, with so slight a barrier between. Imagine the Pope suddenly seated in the midst of Belfast, with the portals of his palace guarded by the doughty, sash-wearing veterans of Dr. Kane and Dr. Hanna, and you have some kind of an idea of the intense antagonism which creates so much of the dramatic interest of the situation at Rome. Imagine, farther, a deputation from the Catholics of Dublin waiting upon the Holy Father to protest their unalterable determination to do their utmost to help him to have, as his ancient and traditional right, the mass celebrated in the church of Dr. Hanna, and you can form some notion of the effect produced on both camps by the advent of these Frenchmen, who, with banners and badges, and no end of episcopal benedictions, have come to the tomb of the Apostles to pay their homage at the feet of the Pope-King. Everything seems tending to a violent issue of the long controversy between Leo and Humbert. The Italians protest, no doubt truly enough, that they will not make a single movement of any kind to precipitate the long-expected solution. But they expect that it will come in spite of their policy of quiescence, and they do not pretend to lament the coming of a crisis which would enable them to get rid, once for all, of the enemy within their gates. The pilgrims protest that their mission is in no sense political. I saw yesterday the son of M. Harmel, who is the organiser of the pilgrimage, and nothing could be more explicit than his account of the spirit which prompted this great popular demonstration. "If you ask me personally," he said, "whether I think that it would be right to restore the Temporal Power, if needs be by force of arms, I am quite of opinion that it would be right. Nay, more, I personally would be glad to fight and die in so glorious a cause. But that is only a personal opinion. The pilgrims have not come to make war or to demand anything political. They come simply and solely to testify their sympathy, their affection, and their devotion to the Head of the Church." This is no doubt true. But the Crusades began in pilgrimages. And the wars which drenched the East with blood had their origin in the pious promenades of the faithful to the Holy Sepulchre. History may not repeat itself; but if the Italian Government were to forbid the influx of thousands of able-bodied Frenchmen who come to acclaim the Pope-King within the kingdom of King Humbert, who can say what consequences might not ensue?

Sunday at Rome is not, to the wayfaring man who sojourns for a time in the city of the Cæsars and of the Popes, very Sabbatical. You miss most of all the peals of church bells which in England make the air vibrate with music, and in Russia fill the ear with a deep pathetic harmony of sound. In all this city of churches there is little audible in the early morning but the rattle of the tramcars and cabs, and the unmusical ding-dong of the tin-pot bells, whose hideous monotone would justify the indictment of the bellringer as the creator of a public nuisance. The foliage on the trees in the Pincian Gardens, on which I am looking out as I am writing, is not stained with the crimson of autumn; the sky is as blue as that of an English June; and one of the most curious features—not in the programme of the great reception—was the presence of a few browny-red butterflies, which fluttered over the heads of the pilgrim crowd in the very presence of the Pope. "Poor little thing!" said a sweet-featured Irish man who stood by me in the press. "I wonder if he had his ticket of admission!" It was not of butterflies, however, that the crowd was thinking, as it pressed tumultuously round the frail barrier of the goldfinch-uniformed halberdiers who, with their white plumes and steel helmets, stood like statues in the hall, keeping, as best they could, the enthusiasm of the devout from blocking up the passage down which the Pope was to make his way from his palace-prison to the crimson throne which had been raised in the centre of the hall. "Pilgrims, remember,"

said L'Abbé Séré, who delivered the address to the pilgrims on the eve of their departure—"remember that
the Vatican is not only a prison and a Calvary, it is also
a Sinai, where an infallible word makes itself heard.
For you the Vatican is a veritable Tabor, where the
grace of our Lord and Saviour Jesus Christ will manifest
itself in the person of the successor of Peter." Around
the head of every pilgrim, they were told, there would
develop a dazzling aureole, from the mere fact of their
visit to the Holy Father. Before assembling in the
Vatican on Sunday morning, the faithful had been wound
up to a great pitch of enthusiasm. Some of them had
seen the foot of Saint Theresa; others had been down to
the subterranean passages, where St. Luke is said by tradition to have composed the story of the Acts of the
Apostles; while others that very morning had paid a
pious pilgrimage to the marble effigy that represents the
mortal remains of St. Cecilia, that rest under the altar
in the church of St. Cecilia in the Trastevere. What
with prayers, and hymns, and pilgrimages, they were
excited to the highest point; and hence it was not to be
wondered at that, when the waving plumes of ostrich and
peacock feathers heralded the approach of the scarlet
palanquin in which the Pope was borne through the hall
to the scarlet throne, a wild cry of enthusiasm broke out,
which was kept up with endless repetition during the
whole of the Pontifical progress down the hall. The
Pope, who looked exceedingly well in his scarlet and
ermine-trimmed robes, distributed his blessing to the

right and the left of the applauding multitude. Seated
in his elevated chair, all present had an excellent view of
the Pope, and he was well worth looking at—a fine
figure, admirably suited to play the central rôle in a
great pageant.   There was in his features a look of
mingled sweetness and of triumph, which was noted with
delight by those who rent the air with their plaudits.
The Holy Father was pleased, palpably pleased, at the
tears of his faithful French, and they on their part were
in an ecstasy.   When he changed his gorgeous palanquin
for the simpler sedan chair on which he was borne up
the steps of his throne, the press to touch his person was
almost too great for the halberdiers to withstand.   At
last he was carried off in safety, and duly ensconced
under the scarlet canopy.   Brazen-helmeted guards
stood on each side of the throne, their headgear recalli-
ing curious reminiscences of the Cæsars; the great
ostrich plumes towered aloft, reminding us of Egypt,
while at intervals down the hall gleamed the sharp and
polished steel of the halberds of the Pontifical Guards.   It
was a very striking scene, full of colour and dramatic
effect.

After the Pope was seated, the hall became as silent
as if those who filled it were as dead as their fellow-
believers in the Catacombs.   Then a French Cardinal,
invisible to all but those immediately surrounding the
throne, began to read the address of the French workmen and peasants composing the pilgrimage.   The
voice was not musical, nor was it for the most part

intelligible. The address, however, contained much good sense. It was, roughly and baldly stated, an appeal to the Holy See to play the same excellent rôle in the solution of all social and labour questions throughout the world which Cardinal Manning has played in the dockers' strike. There was, of course, no tactless reference to Cardinal Manning. But the spirit of the address was unmistakable.

The address recalled the fact that but a short time ago the Pope had expressed approval of an international regulation of the conditions of labour, and expressed the utmost confidence that the working classes would find in the Pope and his Church the effective guardian of their rights. There was much that was touching in the address. Lord save us, they cried, or we perish— perish beneath a moral pestilence which has invaded the world of labour, attacking at once morality, justice, human dignity, and domestic life. But how can this pestilence be averted? In old days, when the great Gregory occupied the throne of St. Peter, a pious procession to the Cathedral is said to have had such an effect upon the pestilence, that when they reached the Tiber, the good Pope saw over the Castle of St. Angelo the Archangel Michael sheathing his sword, and the pestilence was stayed. The figure of the angel still stands in bronze on the summit of the old castle; but the French pilgrims had other suggestions to make as to the method of staying the plague which was eating its way into the veins of human society. What they demanded was that the Pope should seek to unite all who care for the welfare of the working man in support of the following legislative programme:—

1. To protect children from early, excessive, and dangerous labour.

2. To restore the mother of the family to her household and domestic duties.

3. To establish the six days' working week; and

4. To secure shorter hours of labour.

The good Frenchmen did not condescend upon particulars as to how these things should be accomplished, but they evidently meant that it should be effected by legislation, and by international legislation. They deplored usurious speculation, and they lamented the constant increase of taxation caused by the armed peace of Europe. Finally, they implored his Holiness to recall the world to the duty of guaranteeing the working man, whose labour is his only resource, the security of his home, the means of providing for his wife and children, to bring them up like Christians, and to make some provision for rainy days. A tolerably comprehensive programme to present to the Pope. If adopted seriously, it would make the Holy See the head centre of a Christian International, and rally the labouring population round the Church as their great stay and defence.

The Cardinal having ended, the Pope began to read his reply. He had written it out on several sheets of foolscap, which he held in both hands as he read it out to the listening crowd.   At first his voice was clearly audible, but soon nothing was heard but a low, indistinct murmur. He gesticulated freely, reading, although inaudibly, with dramatic vehemence, turning from side to side as if to address all portions of the audience in turn.   A good deal of the Pope's speech was only the usual platitudinous commonplace about charity, the obligations of the rich to the poor, and the wickedness of the unbeliever, which, of course, may be taken for granted, like the elaborate compliments with which every Indian prince begins his despatches to the government of India.   Our translators always begin the English version of their correspondence by the words "after compliments," and "after commonplaces" may appropriately condense the first half of Pontifical deliverances.   The Pope did not in so many words accept the rôle of the Socialist leader of the world.   But he is willing to move in that direction, and his speech was plain enough as an intimation of his tendencies.   The following passage is one which, taken in connection with the nature of the address to which it is a reply, and allowing for the evil traditions of intense Conservatism which linger round the Vatican, is significant enough:—

" It is above all things incumbent upon those in power to saturate themselves with this truth, that to exorcise the peril which menaces society, neither human laws, nor the repressive measures of magistrates, nor the arms of soldiers will suffice ; that which is above all things indispensable is that the Church should be free to revive divine precepts in the souls of men—to extend over all classes of society her salutary influence, that by means of regulations and of wise and equitable measures they should guarantee the interests of labour, they should protect youth, the feebleness and *la mission toute domestique de la femme*, the right and duty of Sunday rest, and thereby should encourage in families as in individuals purity of morals and the habits of a well-ordered and Christian life. The public good, not less than justice and natural right, demand that this should be done."

That is the Pope's social programme, and on the whole, although not quite so clearly accentuated as it may yet become, holds out good promise of future development. As the Pope went on to condemn inordinate profits and rapid and disproportionate gains, Leo XIII. seems in a fair way to found a claim to canonisation on an anathema of 10 per cent.

After a concluding wail over his condition, which, although he declared it to be incompatible with real independence, would not hinder him in the least from becoming the leader of the Social Democracy of the world, if he could but forget his yearnings for temporal authority in Rome, the Pope gave us all his blessing. He was then hoisted up into his palanquin, and the Pontifical cortège departed amid great cheers. The pilgrims then crowded to kiss the chair on which the Pope had sat, and rubbed rosaries against the palanquin in which he had been borne through the hall. "They are quite in ecstasy," remarked a Russian to me. But the ecstasy after all was far less wonderful than that which glowed on the faces of the pilgrims whom I saw at Troitsa last year. After all, it is difficult to get up as much steam when you go pilgriming by cheap trip as when you tramp on foot to a shrine across a continent.

To-day we had mass celebrated in the same hall by the Pope. He was a stately figure, and the ceremonial was performed with all the pomp and glory of the Roman rite. He looked extremely well, and went through the service with vigour and apparent ease. His voice after one hour and a half service—for there were two masses, of which he was the celebrant in the first—was clear and unbroken as he pronounced the benediction. The music was good, the congregational singing of the psalm at the close was full of power and feeling. It might have been mistaken for the singing at a good camp-meeting, or at Mr. Spurgeon's, or at one of the Presbyterian churches north of the Border.

The imposing figure at the altar was very fine, and the effect of the burst of sunshine which from time to time streamed in through the great windows over the gilded helmets and the gleaming halberds was very beautiful. After the second mass was ended, the congregation vociferously cheered the Pope, who departed amid general jubilation. The leaders of the pilgrims, who had received Holy Communion from the hands of his Holiness, then marshalled their procession, with all its banners, and the great function was at an end. Who can say, however, when we shall see the end of the impetus which the visit may have given to the Socialist tendencies of the Pope?

The following is a translation of the Address presented to the Holy Father, and read by his Eminence Cardinal Langenieux (Archbishop of Rheims) :—

" Most Holy Father,—I have the signal honour of presenting to your Holiness the first group of the pilgrimage of French workmen, who come to bring to your feet not only an evidence of their faith and of their love, but also a respectful expression of their gratitude, and of their filial confidence in your paternal and all-powerful protection.

" Full sure (both as Christians and as having been reminded of it by your Holiness), full sure, I say, that the Church has always watched with a jealous care over the working classes, that it is she who has ennobled toil and proclaimed it to be meritorious in the eyes of God, they heard with the greatest joy the words of your Holiness two years ago—that this same Church, in those past times when her voice was more carefully listened to and obeyed, came to the aid of the toilers in a far more substantial way than by her charity and largess ; that she created and encouraged those great guilds which have lent such powerful aid to the progress of the arts and manufactures, and procured for the workmen a larger portion of ease and well-being; they heard that she had imposed this ealous care of hers upon all her surroundings of social influence, so that it was observable in the statutes and ordinances of the towns and boroughs, as also in their definitions of the power of the commonwealth.

" Your Holiness has assured us that the Church continues to-day this work of hers in times past. With what an effusion of gratitude did these workmen of ours receive your words, most Holy Father, when you added : ' We will not cease from putting into practice for the amelioration of your lot all that our duty and our paternal heart may suggest to us.'

" And, indeed, it is but some few months since that your Holiness deigned to praise the project of providing, by some international legislation between the industrial peoples of Europe, for the protection of the working class from those evils which make a Christian man suffer most—those of his home.

" Our thanks, Holy Father, in the name of the great family of toilers ! Those who make the lot of the workman their care will unite their efforts to protect young children from the perils of the workshop, to reinstate the mother in her household and in her natural duties, to protect all workers against excessive labour by preventing the extension of the working hours beyond their normal limit, to guarantee the Sunday rest—hoping to be able to thus combat, in an efficacious manner, the moral plague which is insinuating itself into the very blood of human society.

"Yes, Holy Father, we repeat it. A moral plague invades at this hour the whole working world; it attacks at once ' the morality, the right, the human dignity, and the life of the workman '—(comp. letter of Monsignor Jacobini to M. Demitius: 1 Mar., '89)—those four great points which—as your Holiness has declared—should never be attacked or compromised. Every day brings a new and more evident proof of the justice of the judgment passed by your Holiness upon the modern schools of political economy. 'Steeped in unbelief, they consider labour as the supreme end of man—himself a machine of greater or less value according as he is more or less fit for production.'

"It is but the logical result of the present organisation of our society, which reposes no longer on the basis of faith. And the evil is augmented yet more by the burdens imposed upon industry on the part of the continually increasing action of usurious speculation, as well as by constant rise of the taxes, which must obviously be unnaturally swelled in nations which are perpetually in arms one against the other.

"In the face of this situation, which is no creation of theirs, which they are obliged to submit to, and which violence would but accentuate, the working classes, unable either effectually to help their brethren or to obtain adequate representation in the national councils (through the lack of those very guilds which your Holiness has so warmly praised), would be left isolated, abandoned to their own resources, at once desirous and unable to revolt, if they had not recourse to the Church, whose sacred power has always weighed with all its influence in the scale of the Christian Republic —and even in our time—for we have memorable and consoling examples of your Holiness's action in this matter.

"Moreover, Holy Father, while some, under the influence of those egotistical ideas which at present rule the world, seek, in the perpetual antagonism of employer and employed, the remedy for these evils, and consider themselves unable to arrive at a part of their rights but by the upsetting of society—while others, again, hope, by their own individual efforts—generous and persevering, it is true—to put an end to this offence, these workmen, who are now at the feet of your Holiness, and all those whom they represent, submit themselves, as Christians in obedience to God, to the painful consequences of their humble station. They understand that its evils are due not so much to the ill-will of individuals as to the deep-rooted causes of the disorganisation of society—they repudiate the idea of any personal hatred, any attempts against property, any revolt against authority, any recourse to violent means for the amelioration of their lot—but they appeal to the justice of the commonweal, whose province it is to protect the interests of its citizens, and especially of those among them whose weakness renders their need of protection greater. And, lifting their eyes yet higher to that bright summit from which all truth, all civilisation have flowed, they lift their hands and voices to you, Holy Father, in whom they see the Vicegerent of the authority and fatherhood of God, repeating that sublime cry of the Apostles to their Divine Master: *"Domine salva nos, perimus!"*

"Their confidence will not be in vain. They know in whom they have placed their trust. It is in him who has deigned to take in hand the interests not only of nations but of that large class of toilers which is the most numerous of all—those victimised by the violation of the rights of men, and by the militarism of modern times. It was he, indeed, who reminded the powers and their peoples, in the Allocution of last February, that 'The Church softened and humanised the barbarians by communicating to them the laws of justice as a rule for the intercourse of nations, and in laying it down as an obligation for great and small, for rulers and ruled, never to fight in an unjust cause.'

"Your children, Holy Father, have it at heart to thank you for having graciously proclaimed these guardian principles; and full of a filial confidence, they have ventured to beg your Holiness—in spite of the special difficulties of our times—not to flag in recalling to the world its respect for laws, for justice, and for right, in the necessary intercommunication of men, so as to guarantee the labourer, whose toil is his only resource, a stable hearth, an easy provision for his family, its Christian education, and the possibility of making for it some saving against the hard times which the future may have in store.

I

" May your Holiness—so much tried itself by the injustice of
men—associate to its own august cause, so dear to our hearts, the
humble one of its children, and liberally bestow an abundance of
all celestial blessings upon these French workmen, upon their
families, upon their toil, and upon its results."

To which his Holiness Pope Leo XIII. read the
following reply :—

" Two years ago a numerous phalanx of working-men—come
from France—grouped themselves around us on this spot. To them
our year of Jubilee was opening under the happiest auspices, and
they were bringing us the first-fruits, as it were, of the manifesta-
tions of the Catholic world.   That day left a profound and grateful
impression upon our mind, an impression which your presence,
dear children, and the noble words which have just been addressed
to us in your name by his Eminence the Cardinal who leads this
pilgrimage, can but revive and render ineffaceable for ever. Welcome !   The homage which you are paying to the Head of the
Catholic Church at this moment reveals the foundation of your
thoughts.   You have grasped the fact—at once by your hearts and
your intelligences—that in Religion alone can you find consolation
in the midst of your weariness and perpetual miseries here below.
Religion alone, indeed, has the power to present immortal hopes to
your mind.   Religion alone can ennoble your toil, by lifting it to
the level of human dignity and freedom.   Hence it is that you could
give no higher proof of wisdom than is afforded by your confiding
to her your present and your future destinies.   And on this point
we are happy to confirm here the words which we uttered on
another occasion, and which you have just recalled to us.   We
would even insist once again on those truths, persuaded, as we are,
that your welfare, as that of others, depends upon the establishment
in society of the work and teachings of the Church.

" Heathenism, as you know, boasted that it had solved the
social problem, by depriving the weaker portion of humanity of its
rights, by crushing its aspirations, by paralysing its intellectual and
moral faculties, and by reducing it to a state of absolute impotence.
This was slavery.   Christianity came to tell the world that the

entire human family, without any distinctions of patrician and ple-
beian, was called to take part in a divine inheritance; it declared
that all had equal title to be called sons of the Father in Heaven,
that all had been bought by the same price; it taught that labour
was, on this earth, the natural condition of man; that to accept it
with courage was to him an honour and a proof of wisdom; that to
attempt to escape it was at once to show cowardice and to fail in a
sacred and fundamental duty.

"In order to comfort the more efficaciously toilers and the poor,
the Divine Founder of Christianity deigned to add example to His
teachings. He had not where to lay His head; He experienced
the hardships of hunger and thirst; He passed His public and His
private life in weariness, in anguish, and in misery. According to
His doctrine the rich man was, as Tertullian puts it, 'Merely
God's steward upon earth;' to him were addressed the rules concerning temporal goods; to him the Saviour's formidable menaces
if he should harden his heart against the unfortunate and the poor.

"Nevertheless, even this was not enough. It remained to draw
the two classes together, to establish between them an indissoluble
religious bond. For this work came Charity. She created a new
social bond, and gave it a strength and a softness till then unknown;
she furnished by her perpetual increase a remedy for all evils, a
consolation for all pains; and she had the power, through her innumerable works and institutions, to excite a noble and zealous
rivalry in generosity towards the unfortunate.

"Such was the one solution by which, for all the inevitable in-
equality of human stations, life could be rendered supportable. For
centuries this solution was accepted universally, and on all universally imposed. Without doubt there took place beneath it, now
and again, acts of insubordination and revolt; but they were always
local and apart. Faith was too deep-rooted in men's minds for a
general and definitive eclipse to be then possible. No one would
have dreamt of questioning the legitimacy of this foundation of
society; no one would have dared the vast task of its perversion, of
disturbing upon this point the minds and hearts of the people, of
attempting the total ruin of the common weal. As for the nature of
those ill-starred doctrines and events which afterwards ruined the
edifice so patiently raised by the Church, we have mentioned it

elsewhere—we will not come back to it now. What we demand is a new cohesion of its parts, a new stability of that building, to be arrived at by a return to the spirit and doctrines of Christianity, in the revival in all their essentials, in their various practical virtues, and in whatever forms the times allow—those industrial guilds which of old, steeped in Christian thought and inspired by the maternal solicitude of the Church, provided for the religious and material needs of the workmen, eased their toil, guarded their savings, defended their rights, and insisted, in righteous measure, upon their legitimate complaints. What we demand is that, by a sincere return to the principles of Christianity, there should be re-established between master and man, between capital and labour, that harmony and union which is the unique bulwark for the safety of their mutual interests, and upon which depend at once private welfare and public tranquillity and peace.

"Round about you, my dear children, thousands of other toilers are afoot, who, seduced by false doctrines, think to find a remedy for their ills in laying low that which is, as it were, the very essence of civil and political life,—in the destruction and annihilation of property. Vain dreams! They will throw themselves against a wall of immovable laws which nothing can destroy. They will but incarnadine their way, strew it with ruins, sow in it anarchy and discord, and in this act will only aggravate their own miseries, and call upon themselves the curses of honest men. No. The remedy is to be found neither in the perverse and subversive aims and actions of these, nor in the seductive but erroneous theories of those others; it lies entirely in the faithful accomplishment of those duties which are incumbent upon all classes of society—in the respect and maintenance of the attributes and functions proper to each in particular. These truths, these duties, it is the mission of the Church to proclaim aloud and to inculcate to all.

"There must be heart and bowels of compassion among the ruling classes for those who gain their bread by the sweat of their brow; a curb must be put upon their insatiable greed of wealth, of luxury, and of pleasures, which, both above and below, still increases and spreads. In all ranks is to be found this thirst for pleasure, and as all cannot satisfy it, there results a vast discontent, which can only breed perpetual revolt and insurrection.

"Upon the holders of power it is incumbent above all to possess themselves of this truth, that to conjure the perils which menace society, neither human laws, nor the repression exercised by judges, nor the very arms of the soldiery will suffice; that the most important, the indispensable thing, is the liberty of the Church to revive the divine precepts in the souls of men, and to extend its salutary influence to every class. This influence, in conjunction with equitable and wise measures, makes a guarantee for the interests of the working classes; the protection of youth, and of the weakness and peculiarly domestic sphere of womanhood; the right and the duty of the Sunday rest; and it maintains the guardianship both in families and in individuals of purity of morals and of the habits of an orderly and Christian life. The public weal, as also justice and natural right, cry out for such a state of things.

"To masters the rule is laid down that they regard the workman as a brother; that they make his lot easier by all practical limits and equitable conditions; to see both to his temporal and to his spiritual welfare; to edify him by the example of a Christian life, and above all, never to leave, to his hurt, the way of equity and justice in a mad race for rapid profits and ill-proportioned gain.

"With you, on your part, my dear children, it is incumbent, as indeed to all in your position, to lead lives which shall be always worthy of praise by their faithful practice of religious, domestic, and social duties. You told us just now (and it rejoiced us greatly), you told us that it was your formally expressed desire to remain submissive to labour and to its painful consequences; to be always peaceful and respectful towards your employers, whose mission it is to procure you work and to organise it; to abstain from any act capable of disturbing peace and order; to preserve, in fine, and to nourish in your hearts sentiments of gratitude and filial confidence in the Church, which delivered you from the old yoke of slavery and oppression—as also to the Vicar of Jesus Christ, who unceasingly watches over you as a father, to learn your needs and to help them, remind all of their respective duties, and speak to them in the tongue of charity.

"Let that sentiment of gratitude and devotion to the Church and its head remain unshakeable in you and increase from more to more. Yearly does our position become more acute, and the necessity of a real independence and true liberty in the exercise of our apostolic mission becomes more and more evident. As good Catholics, remain faithful, my dear children, to this most noble cause. Do your best, and let each do it in his own sphere, in its defence and for its speedy triumph.

"And now, dear children, go back into your country, into that France where, notwithstanding all its individual and passing errors, I have never seen the ardour for good grow less or the flame of generosity and self-sacrifice pale. Go back to your homes, and prove by your conduct that in these associations where the religious principle reigns, reign also with it brotherly love, peace, sobriety, discipline, the spirit of household thrift and economy. Go, and may the grace of the Lord accompany you everywhere, assist you, protect you, sustain you in your weariness, encourage you in giving you a foretaste, even here, of the ineffable joys which flow from virtue, and which give hope of a better life in the Fatherland of all who believe.

"It is with eyes and hands lifted up to heaven that we raise, that we will raise daily, for you, dear children, such desires, such supplications, and such prayers ; meanwhile, and as an earnest of those heavenly favours, we accord you the Apostolic Benediction, we bless you, all you here present, with all the warmth of our heart, —which is a father's ; we bless your wives—your children—your families. We bless your chiefs, your masters, those who do you good—as also all the pious congregations to which you may belong."

CHAPTER IX.

THE POPE AND THE SOCIAL QUESTION.

IF the Vatican is once more to lead the modern world, it will have to come into touch with it. It will have to know its facts, to be familiar with its problems, to master its difficulties, and to enter with discernment and sympathy into all the phenomena of life. In other words, the Church will have to do in Christendom what it does outside Christendom. If it is to regain its old position, it must do it by the old way. He who would be chief must be servant of all. If it would win back the mind of the age to a realising faith in the love of God, it must convince the unbeliever of the reality of its love for man. No Church which, in Longfellow's fine phrase, is not as lofty as the love of God, and wide as are the wants of man, can ever hope to be universal. Any real need of humanity neglected by the Church creates a schism for which the Church itself is primarily responsible. That Church will most speedily gather the human race within its borders which is most helpful to the human race. The growth of religions is but one continuous application of the great doctrine *Do ut des*.

Give, and it shall be given unto you, is the divine law, from which not even the successor of St. Peter can be exempt.

How came Christianity to transform the world? Because Christians found in their faith a spring of energy sufficient to induce them to die gladly, in order that they might help and save the meanest and worst of their enemies. They brought brotherhood to the slave, help to the sick, food to the starving, and the infinite radiance of an eternal hope into the lives of men. If the Church can do the same to-day in similar measure, its triumph is assured. But is it possible? I do not see any impossibility. The two great factors remain the same. Humanity is still sick at heart and sore of limb. The boundless aspirations of the human heart are no more satisfied by the negations of modern materialism than they were when the followers of the Nazarene were burnt as torches to illumine the gardens on the site of which St. Peter's now stands. And if there be not that love of God which led the early Christians to lay down their lives for the brethren, that assuredly is not because mankind cannot appreciate such testimony, but because love has grown cold in the heart of the Church. Of Churches, as of individuals, it may be said that they enter into the kingdom prepared from the foundations of the world, or are cast into outer darkness, exactly as to the least of these My brethren they fulfil or neglect the simple duties of brotherly love. "I was an hungered, and ye gave me meat: I was thirsty, and ye gave me drink: I was a stranger, and ye took me in: naked, and ye clothed me: I was sick, and ye visited me: I was in prison, and ye came unto me." It is the supreme test alike of the Supreme Judge at the last assize, and of the vulgar, selfish creatures who make up the mass of mankind. Whatever may be said as to the root of the tree which bears such useful fruit, it is the fruit that convinces the outsider, who is quite as unceremonious with Churches which bear nothing but the leaves of ceremonial and rites as was Jesus of Nazareth with the barren fig-tree.

When I was on my way to Rome, hurrying south-ward along the line that leads from Pisa to Rome, the train was suddenly drawn up with a jerk that threw us from our seats. As we rushed to the windows, the bitter wail of a woman's voice rang horribly through the silent night. A moment more, and we could see her pacing backwards and forwards, wringing her hands, and crying aloud in the very frenzy of passionate despair. We were at a level crossing. Her husband, who was trying to lead his horse and cart across the line, had been run over. The horse without its master stood motionless as a statue in the shafts, gazing stolidly at the train that lay across its path. It was black night; in the neighbour-ing houses we could see the lighted windows, and not a quarter of a mile off we could discern dimly the dark outline of a village through the trees. The only sound was that woman's cry of agony. After a pause, the search commenced. The body of the unfortunate man

was found under the carriages at the rear of the train.
When he was extricated he was breathing. Blood was
streaming from a great wound on his brow, and although
but barely conscious, he did not appear to have suffered
any mutilation. They were going to lay the poor wretch
on the ground, when an old English resident in Italy,
who happened to be in the train, interfered, and succeeded in getting him placed on a truckle bed in the
wayside cabin. But there our resources seemed to dis-
appear. The woman wailed on. A group of curious
passengers gathered round the wounded man, who might
at any moment breathe his last. A couple of priests
hurried up, ready to administer consolation to the dying.
But of intelligent, practical, helpful human service there
was next to none. Instead of putting him into the train
and carrying him on to the station, which was not ten
minutes off, where he might have found a doctor and a
nurse, there was a general jabbering and gesticulating ;
then we all took our seats, and the train moved on,
leaving the poor bleeding wretch to his fate. Whether
he recovered, or whether he succumbed to his injuries, no
one knew. As we slowly steamed away the woman was
still wringing her hands, and the masterless horse still
stood motionless in the roadway. A moment more and
they were left behind in the black and silent night.
There was no lack of kindly sentimental sympathy
among the passengers, but they were utterly at a loss
how to give it effect. There was no one to take the lead,
to initiate, to direct. And therein, the more I think of

that sombre scene, the more does it appear to be an
only too grimly faithful illustration of our present social
state. Down beneath the wheels of our industrial civilisation, bruised and bleeding, but still conscious, lies the
luckless proletaire. The bitter cry of his helpless women-
folk pierces the silence, but no one knows what to do, or
how to help. Spiritual consolation is not wanting in
case he were to die; but of intelligent, effective assistance, to enable him to live, there is next to none. We
stand and chatter, and express unavailing sympathy for a
time, and then we hurry on, leaving him to his fate.

It is not want of good feeling. It is lack of direction,
the absence of intelligent understanding of what ought
to be done and how to do it. The world is full of such
instances, and would welcome only too eagerly any
organisation which brought sagacity and enlightened
sympathy to the assistance of those who have not where-
withal to lead a human life. This is the supreme test
which is being applied, not merely to the Roman
Church, but to all Churches and all civilisations. It
would be intolerance of the worst kind to refuse to hail
with anxious welcome the faint but unmistakable indica-
tions which the present Pope has given of his desire to
realise the duty that is incumbent upon all Christian
men. He may be but half awake to the pressing importance of the social question. But he is groping
eagerly forward, and it would be treason to humanity to
bid him stand aside and cease his efforts, merely because
he wears a three-crowned hat and claims to hold the

keys of Heaven in his grasp. We shall doubt less his claims to hold the keys of Heaven if he succeeds in making this world a little less of a hell. Therein lies the only path by which he can regain his supremacy of influence over the lives and the hearts of men.

When Gregory the Great was told one day that a solitary unknown beggar had been found dead from starvation in the streets of Rome, he excommunicated himself for having allowed such a thing to happen in a city under his rule. For days he abstained from communion, shutting himself up in his silent cell, to make atonement by tears and penance for his sin of omission towards that poor starveling. If Leo the Thirteenth can imbue his clergy throughout the world with something of the spirit that drove St. Gregory to his penitential cell, he will soon have cause to forget the miserable temporalities of his departed kingdom in the glories of the Empire which he will found in the love and affection of mankind. Whether he or any of his successors will prove equal to this high emprise who can venture to say? For my own part I am disposed to hope. The destruction of the Temporal Power has abolished that which was the chief obstacle in the way of the Church allying itself frankly and sincerely with the common people. And the tribulation which the Pope has had to suffer from the Italian Government has been calculated to rid the Holy See of many inveterate fallacies, which rendered it practically useless as an instrument of social reform. There is no teaching like that of experience to enlighten the Church as to the absurdity of its fetish worship of authority and of material force. The cant of legality—as if an injustice became one whit more tolerable because it was consecrated by a law—is being pretty severely shaken to pieces in the mind of the Pope by the legislation of the Italian Government. The Pope and his counsellors, after centuries of domination, have now begun to learn what it is to be under the harrow of oppression. It will make them more sympathetic with sufferers all over the world, and more ready to look behind the letter of parchment law to the justice or injustice of the edict against which human beings are rising in revolt. The successive confiscations to which the Church has been subjected will tend in the same direction. A Church that is groaning under the weight of its treasures cannot be trusted to defend the cause of the poor against the rich. Not until, as in Ireland, it is the poverty-stricken Church of the poor, can it really become the tribune of the people, and vindicate with hearty sympathy the rights of the down-trodden and oppressed against their wealthy and insolent oppressors.

While the ultimate aim of the Church must ever be to teach men to lead the divine life, it is one of the most promising signs of the times that the Holy See is beginning to use the organization at its disposal to help men to secure the conditions of a human existence. Nothing can be more certain than that the Holy Father is a Socialist at heart—a sanctified Socialist, no doubt, but one who is bent upon realising as much Socialism as

can be obtained within the limits of the Ten Com-
mandments. His zeal, it may be, is not according to
knowledge. He is surrounded by Congregations or
managing committees, who are competent to advise him
upon all manner of things ecclesiastical and theological.
But he has no consulters worth speaking of who can give
him help or guidance in dealing with the complicated
phenomena of social and industrial life. He is a theorist,
a philosopher, rather than a practical man, and, like all
idealists, is apt to imagine that he can rush in where men
of experience would fear to tread. But when he comes
to deal with the social question seriously, he will find
that it is not a matter to be disposed of in the platitudes
of an Encyclical, or by the pious aspirations of a devout
soul. He has first to recognise his limitations, which
after all are the conditions of his strength, and then to
discover the direction in which he can most effectively
utilise the unique advantages of his position. The be-
setting temptation of the Holy See is to imagine that it
has a peculiar dispensation which exempts it from the
necessity of taking the same pains to avoid blunders
which are obvious to all who do not dwell in the atmosphere of infallibility. As a result, the Pope, with
the best intentions in the world, makes blunders which
react disastrously upon his prestige. There is something almost pathetic in the fatuity of his action in
relation to the social question in Ireland. There, if
anywhere, it might have been expected that he would
have avoided the mistakes into which he actually fell.

His condemnation of the subscription to Mr. Parnell, and his famous "Rescript" condemning boycotting and the Plan of Campaign, may have been intrinsically right or intrinsically wrong. Of that I say nothing. What is certain is, that in both cases his Holiness neglected to take the most ordinary precautions needful to ascertain the facts of the case upon which he was pronouncing, and as a result be excited in the most devoted Catholics in Christendom an angry suspicion that the Holy See had been tampered with. The more I dive into the secret history of the Persico "Rescript," the more utterly incomprehensible does it appear. To launch a bolt from the blue in that fashion, contrary to the urgent counsel of the trusted envoy whom you had deputed to examine into the subject on the spot, and without even waiting to hear a single word of explanation from your own Irish Archbishop, who was actually in attendance in the Papal antechamber in order to explain the action which you are about to condemn, is conduct that justifies a considerable misgiving as to whether the Holy See is likely to be more of a blessing than a nuisance in the field of social reform. The Pope, however, has had a lesson. He also has learned something of the need for Home Rule. In future he will do nothing of that sort without at least hearing the views of the Irish and American bishops. That prudent resolve, if resolutely adhered to and logically carried out in other directions, will enable him to avoid many pitfalls into which he would otherwise have

plunged headlong.   After all, it does not require a divine
revelation to recognise that a competent and conscientious
bishop on the spot, familiar with all the local circumstances, and face to face with all the practical difficulties,
is more likely to see where the line of wisdom and
justice lies than the greatest Pope who ever sat in the
chair of St. Peter—a very high seat, no doubt, but one
which does not give its occupant eyes that see unto the
ends of the earth.   The autocratic associations of the
Cæsars still haunt the Imperial city.   The idea of
centralisation is one of the most inveterate of the moral
miasmas of Rome.   Of course, if the Pope could claim
special divine revelation, affording him infallible guidance
both as to the facts and as to the judgment to be pronounced on those facts, there could be no more to be
said.   But as not even the most extravagant infallibilist
ventures to make such a claim, the Pope will find, like
other great secular Governments, that decentralisation
is the condition of efficiency, and even of existence.
Home Rule is the key to the solution of other problems
than those of the British Empire.   The Pope, no doubt,
will have his uses, even when the affairs of each province
of the Catholic world are left largely to the guidance of
the local hierarchy.   But the allowance of a larger
liberty to the local churches in all matters social and
political is the indispensable condition of any intelligent
direction of the moral force of Catholicism.

If the Pope abandoned the attempt to steer the ship
from the shore—the common delusion of mortals who

have never been to sea—he would be able to devote his
attention more profitably to drawing up sailing directions,
and imparting to his representatives all over the world
the impetus of his social and humanitarian enthusiasm.
There is still plenty of room in the campaign against the
ills of the world for an international Director-General of
the Humanitarian forces of the world. As the world
shrinks, becoming every day, under the plastic influences of steam and electricity, more and more one
vast parish of cosmopolitan humanity, the need for an
international centre for common action towards common
ends becomes more and more apparent. The Pope
may be in many respects unfitted to occupy that central
post; but he has at least the aspiration to occupy it, and
no mortal starts with greater advantages. If he can but
inspire mankind with a sense of his absolute impartiality
and his unswerving justice, not all the top hamper of
his ecclesiastical paraphernalia and theological mysteries
will prevent his arrival. This may seem a vain dream to
many who profess to believe much more in the Holy
See than is possible to a Protestant, to whom the
dogma of Infallibility and the spiritual pretensions of
the Pope are simply incredible. But the fact is there.
Mankind hungers and craves for guidance; we ask
only to be led instead of being driven. Authority of
the Old Order, established by miracle and enforced
by the rack and the stake, has vanished from the
world. But authority in the New Era, which speaks
with the voice of reason, which is established on an

K

incontrovertible basis of established facts, and is supported by the tangible evidence of great secular services
rendered by its means, will find mankind only too
willing to obey. Human progress has shivered the
old sceptre in the hands of the Pope, but it has left
him free to grasp the new sceptre which is visibly
within his reach.

Will he grasp it? That is the question which I
have been discussing all day and every day ever since
I came to Rome. He would like to, and yet he is
afraid. Not without cause. Who can say what might
follow if so much exceedingly new wine were poured
into the old bottles? And yet that fear is but a
phase of unbelief. Humanity, wandering forlorn in the
Wilderness of Sin, cries aloud for a new Moses to lead it
across the desert to the Promised Land of the new
social order. It is not for the Vicar of Christ to shrink
back dismayed from the responsibility of answering to
that call. Leo XIII. is not indisposed to attempt the
great duty. He sees that the supreme chance for the
Church lies in contributing to the solution of the social
question. But here, again, comes upon him the second
phase of the temptation in the wilderness. He is dis·
posed to trust in his infallibility to guide him aright,
and to rely upon the Divine guidance to prevent his
falling into disastrous mistakes, instead of carefully avail-
ing himself of all the simple and commonplace precautions which ordinary mortals know must be taken if
they are to judge justly, act wisely, and give helpful

counsel. Like his Master, the Pope has been taken up into the holy city and set on a pinnacle of the Temple, while the tempter whispers in his ear that he should cast himself down, for it is written, "He shall give His angels charge concerning thee, and in their hands they shall bear thee up, lest at any time thou shalt dash thy foot against a stone." It is the old story of the Temptation of Presumption. We shall see before long if the Pope can thrust it by.

CHAPTER X.

THE POPE AND MR. PARNELL.

To us in England Ireland is the touchstone of the Papal claims to play a beneficent rôle in the solution of the social question. I need not here discuss the part played by Leo XIII. in German politics, where his intervention in support of Prince Bismarck's Military Law met the stout resistance of German Catholics, and excited fierce indignation in France. That does not concern us. Ireland does. There we see the Papal engine in practical operation. What has the Vatican done for the Irish peasant?

This question brings me to the heart of the subject— viz., whether the non-Catholic peoples can be induced to believe that the Holy See is to be relied upon to exercise an efficacious and continuous influence on behalf of the peoples, especially on behalf of the labouring classes.

Before the Holy Father can make himself the international centre of all efforts made to solve the social question, by the amelioration of the lot of the workman and the peasant, he has to overcome a great obstacle in the shape of a suspicion that he cannot be relied upon to

act as the tribune of the common people, impartially
vindicating the rights of the poor, and insisting with an
authoritative voice upon their just claims. Among
English Liberals there are few who have not arrived at
the conclusion that it is impossible to place any such
reliance in the Holy See. This conclusion is one which
has been forced upon us by the melancholy experience
of Ireland.

If ever there was any province of the Christian
Church in which the Holy See might have been expected
to exert a beneficial influence on the solution of the social
question, Ireland is that country. There the people and
their priests are as one. The priest is the father, the
leader, the tribune of his flock. Nowhere is there a
population more devoted to the Catholic faith and to the
discharge of their religious duties. The social question
arose there in its acutest form when the peasantry, confronted by the horrors of eviction and of starvation,
united with their priests to demand from their landlords
and from the English Government some relief in the
shape of a juster land-tenure and reduced rents.

The justice of these claims was indisputable. Tardily
it has been recognised by the landlords and by the
Government, chiefly owing to the exertions of Mr. Parnell, to whom a grateful nation, led by its Episcopate and
its priesthood, was rendering substantial thanks, when
suddenly the Holy See interfered. During the long
struggle of the peasants for justice and even for life, the
Holy Father was practically dumb. When at last Rome

spoke with decisive voice, it spoke not to support but to condemn the leader of the Irish race in their struggle for liberty, for justice, and for the means of subsistence. The letter " De Parnellio " was a cruel reminder of the fact that, although the Holy Father may be infallibly inspired, he is not always infallibly informed. Nor is the Holy See beyond the range of political influences not always of the highest kind.

That is not the only instance of the same sort. The " Plan of Campaign," devised by Irish patriots for the defence of the scanty property of Irish tenants, threatened with confiscation by landlords who took advantage of a bad season or a fall in prices to seize their holdings, was publicly approved by the Archbishop of Dublin. Dr. Walsh knew the facts. He was on the spot. He was a prelate honoured with the confidence of the Holy See, which conferred upon him the Archbishopric of Dublin. But notwithstanding all this, notwithstanding the confidence which his appointment had revived in the Irish heart with regard to the benevolent disposition of the Holy See, the famous Rescript was issued, condemning the " Plan of Campaign " as contrary to morality, and covering with shame the face of the Archbishop. Never can I forget the howl of exultant joy which rose from the enemies of Ireland over the unexpected intervention of the Holy See in opposition to the cause of the people. They openly boasted that the Pope was now in the pocket of the English Government, that Rome supported the English ascendency against the Irish Catholic bishops and the suffering peasantry. The decisions of the Holy See in those cases were undoubtedly prompted by the desire of the Holy See to keep the Irish within the bounds of legality. Yet, by a strange irony, the condemnation of the Holy See was directed against the men who in ten years had done more to substitute legal, open, and constitutional action for the criminal practices of secret societies than the Church herself had been able to effect in a century.

With two such incidents fresh in our memory, can it be wondered at that we regard with considerable misgiving the action of the Holy See in dealing with the social question elsewhere?

For Ireland is the great mainstay of the Church in the great English-speaking world. Every day the number, the strength, the wealth of the English-speaking nations increase and multiply. Europe dwindles; the New World grows greater and greater; and the Catholic soul of all these nations, whether in England, Scotland, America, Australia, New Zealand, or South Africa, is Irish. Without the Irish the English-speaking world would be almost exclusively Protestant. It is the Irish who, in the New World, are the real and living force "De Propaganda Fide;" yet, so far at all events as persons outside the Church can possibly form any consistent view of what was done, it must be regarded by them as a sacrifice of their interests by Rome when they came into collision with the interests of the wire-pullers and the emissaries of the wealthy and powerful English.

If the Holy See can thus disregard the claims of the most faithful of its children, how can it expect to command the confidence of the non-Catholic peoples, without whose co-operation the social question can never be solved?

The more closely the action of the Holy See is looked into in those matters, the more deplorable and . inexplicable becomes the conduct of the Pope. I have discussed the matter with high and low in Rome, and I am as much as ever at a loss to understand how the Pope could be so blind to his own interests, and to the obvious justice of the claims of the Irish. The only suggested explanation is, that the Irish suffer for their loyalty. They are so submissive, so humble, so reluctant to tell the Pope unpalatable truths, that he falls into the hands of those who have no such scruples, and who do not hesitate to use every means at their disposal for securing the Pope's attention to their representations. Never can I forget the bitter sadness of the tone of one good Catholic Irishman with whom I walked across the Piazza di Spagna. "Never," said he with intense feeling, "never is it possible for the voice of truth about Ireland to penetrate the Vatican. For a hundred years it has always been the same. You know how O'Connell was treated. Ireland has been nothing at Rome, and an Irishman has been nothing because Ireland was nothing. Unless, indeed," he added bitterly, " unless he betrayed his country; then he was everything. But why should we care about that lot up at the Vatican?

What do they know of our affairs? What do they
know about Ireland? They have got to earn their living
like the rest of us, and they like to do it the easiest way
they can." If that is the nett result of the experience of
the most devoted Catholic province in all the world, it
is a poor look-out for the rest of us. If there is one man
in Ireland who represents the social question, that man
is Michael Davitt. He is at once a leader of the people
and a devoted Catholic. Yet when he was at Rome he
was scouted as if he had been an assassin, and his advice
and information were never utilised at the Vatican.
Before starting for Rome I asked Mr. Davitt what he
would say if he were asked by the Holy See what the
Pope could do for Ireland. His reply was as follows :—

" This is the substance of what I would say, in more diplomatic
language, of course, if, as you say, the Holy Father were to deem
it worth his while to ask my opinion on the matter :

" Ireland is to-day the great Propagandist of the Catholic faith.
Irish bishops and priests rule the Catholic Church throughout the
English-speaking world. Irish emigrants have taken the seeds of the
faith into England, Scotland, Wales, America, Canada, South Africa,
Australia. This missionary work has never been recognised at the
centre of the Christian world. Ireland's enemies have been more
than once on the point of poisoning your ear against the most
devoted of Catholic nations, simply because you have never commanded your faithful Irish people to send you an accredited representative to reside in Rome, and advise you from time to time
regarding Irish political or social movements, and their real bearing
upon religion and morals. For want of such an unofficial Nuncio,
there has been twice in recent years a narrow escape of a conflict
between the whole Irish race and your Headship of its national
Church. Thoroughly Catholic as the Irish are, they are equally
Nationalist, and will never allow their fidelity to the Catholic faith

to be presumed upon with reference to their Nationalist cause. A pronounced hostility to Home Rule by your Holiness would strike a bigger blow at the Catholic Church throughout the English-speaking world than Luther's revolt did in Germany. Guard against the possibility of this, therefore, by asking the Irish bishops to send, on the behalf of the Irish Catholic race, an accredited representative to reside near your person in Rome, and give him the dignity of a Cardinal in compliment to the race which to-day is making the Church truly universal."

When I was in the Vatican I pressed this point as strongly as I could. But Ireland is too far removed from the centre of the Papal system to be regarded of sufficient importance to have a special representative at Rome. There is Monsignor Kirby, the saintly Rector of the Irish College, one of the best men in Rome, and one of the most thoroughgoing Nationalists, who kneels with his students every day in the Church where lies the heart of O'Connell, and that, they say at the Vatican, is enough. But although no one who knows Monsignor Kirby can help loving him, and although it goes sorely against the grain to say even one word which might possibly grieve that aged saint, Dr. Kirby would be the first to admit that one who has not been in Ireland for forty years, and who is now nearly ninety years of age, is at a great disadvantage in interpreting the latest phases of the agrarian agitation to his old schoolmate, the Pope. The record of the Pope's dealings with Ireland shows that it is necessary to have in Rome an Irishman who, for the sake of the people and the Church of Ireland, would offer, if need be, as uncompromising an opposition to the Tory

entourage of the Holy Father as ever Mr. Parnell offered
to the English Government in the House of Commons.
Such a bold, uncompromising exponent of the truth
about Ireland would have saved the Pope from two of
the most awkward mistakes of his reign.

The first was that in which he condemned the testimonial to Mr. Parnell. In Rome this is generally
ascribed to the influence of Sir George Errington. But
why the Pope should have suffered himself to be led by
Sir George Errington is a mystery past finding out; for
Leo the Thirteenth had bestowed upon Ireland and
Irish affairs much closer attention than many an English
statesman. Some years ago he had told Archbishop
Croke that he was as good an Irishman as himself, and
that he sincerely wished well to his Irish children no
one could doubt who ever met him. In conversations
with Archbishop Walsh he had completely reassured
that prelate as to the genuine sympathy with which
he regarded the Irish cause. So notorious were
his tendencies, that Cardinal Howard, being asked on
one occasion by an Irishwoman whether the Pope
would receive her, replied that there was no doubt of it,
but that if she would say that she was a Home Ruler
his Holiness would receive her with special favour. In
this there is nothing surprising. Ireland is to the future
of Catholicism what England has been to the Protestant
world. Ireland has always been the Isle of the Saints;
but few Englishmen understand that in the new world
which is springing up around us the Irish are the

missionary race.   In a remarkable sermon which Bishop
Vaughan preached many years ago in Rome, he brought
out with extraordinary effect this too often unnoticed
feature of the Irish character.   The Irish brogue is as
universal as the English language, and wherever there is
the brogue there also is the Mass.

Leo the Thirteenth must therefore feel intensely
interested in the somewhat sombre fortunes of his
missionary nation.   But as he plaintively told Cardinal
M'Cabe in 1882, "the condition of Ireland gives him
more anxiety than comfort."   Again and again during
his pontificate he has addressed letters to the Irish
hierarchy, in which it is easy to discern the uneasiness
and uncertainty with which he addresses himself to the
solution of this thorny problem.   Not even to the
successor of St. Peter is vouchsafed that divine illumina-
tion whereby the Irish question can be understood.
However infallible may be the guidance vouchsafed to
the Supreme Pontiff in matters of faith and morals, in
dealing with the complex political and social questions
involved in the Irish question he is sometimes, like all
the rest of us, but as a child groping in the dark.   Like
less exalted mortals, the Holy Father can only act upon
information received.   So far as can be judged from the
documents contained in "*De Rebus Hiberniæ nuperrima
Apostolicæ sedis Acta*"—a collection of Papal letters
and other documents on the Irish question, published as a
pamphlet in 1883 or 1884—he is ill at ease on the subject.
He sees no light.   He is dissatisfied with the existing

condition of the country, but he had implicit confidence
in Mr. Gladstone's Administration. Even when the
Irish gaols had been crammed with untried prisoners,
and Mr. Gladstone was plunging from the Coercion Act
of Mr. Forster to the Coercion Act of Sir W. Harcourt,
the Pope did not hesitate to express his confidence that
the statesmen who preside over the administration of
Ireland would give satisfaction to the Irish when they
demand what is just. He believed in the justice of
those who ruled Ireland, "whose great experience is
generally tempered with judgment." Hence he deprecated excited feelings, and exhorted the people to follow
none but moderate and just counsels, to obey their
bishops, and not to fail in the religious observance of
their duty. He is earnestly anxious for the welfare of
Ireland, but he adds that it is not lawful to disturb
order on account of it. Beyond the issue of more or
less ineffective exhortations to moderation, which fell
idly upon the ears of men whose own bishops declared,
with a far clearer insight into the necessities of the
situation, that energetic action was sounder policy, the
Pope did not venture upon any more drastic measures
than to interdict the younger clergy from taking part in
public meetings—an interdict which is practically a
dead letter.

In May, 1883, however, the Pope ventured to take a
further step. Mr. Parnell's estate in Wicklow being
mortgaged, it was suggested by Archbishop Croke, as a
practical reply to Mr. Forster's attack on the Irish leader

in the House of Commons, that a public subscription should be raised to present him with a testimonial of sufficient money to pay off the mortgage. Archbishop Croke subscribed £50. Nine other Bishops and 200 parish priests followed suit. The movement attained considerable proportions, when suddenly the Pope intervened, urged thereto by Sir George Errington, and condemned the testimonial in the famous letter from the Prefect of the Propaganda to the Bishops of Ireland, which, translated, is as follows :—

"QUALECUMQUE DE PARNELLIO.

" Whatever may be the case as regards Mr. Parnell himself and his objects, it is at all events proved that many of his followers have on many occasions adopted a line of conduct in open contradiction to the rules laid down by the Supreme Pontiff in his letter to the Cardinal Archbishop of Dublin, and contained in the instructions sent to the Irish Bishops by this Sacred Congregation, and unanimously accepted by them at their present meeting at Dublin. It is true that, according to these instructions, it is lawful for the Irish to seek redress for their grievances and to strive for their rights ; but always at the same time observing the Divine maxim, to seek first the Kingdom of God and His justice, and remembering also that it is wicked to further any cause, no matter how just, by illegal means.

" It is therefore the duty of all the clergy, and especially the bishops, to curb the excited feelings of the multitude, and to take every opportunity with timely exhortation to recall them to the justice and moderation which are necessary in all things, that so they may not be led away by greed of gain to mistake evil for good, or to place their hopes of public prosperity in the shame of criminal acts. Hence it follows that it is not permitted to any of the clergy to depart from these rules themselves, or to take part in or in any way to promote movements inconsistent with prudence and with the duty of calming men's minds. It is certainly not forbidden to collect for relief of distress in Ireland; but, at the same time, the aforesaid apostolic mandates absolutely condemn such collections as are raised in order to inflame popular passions, and to be used as means for leading men into rebellion against the laws. Above all things, they (the clergy) must hold themselves aloof from such subscriptions, when it is plain that hatred and dissensions are aroused by them; that distinguished persons are loaded with insults; that never in any way are censures pronounced against the crimes and murders with which wicked men stain themselves; and especially when it is asserted that the measure of true patriotism is in proportion to the amount of money given or refused, so as to bring the people under the pressure of intimidation.

"*Quibus positis*, it must be evident to your lordships that the collection called the 'Parnell Testimonial Fund' cannot be approved by this Sacred Congregation; and consequently it cannot be tolerated that any ecclesiastic, much less a bishop, should take any part whatsoever in recommending or promoting it.

"Meanwhile we pray God long to preserve your lordship.

"Rome, May 11, 1883."

The immediate result of the publication of this Papal thunderbolt was the doubling of the subscription list. The utmost that it was believed could be raised for Mr. Parnell was £20,000 before the Papal ban. The moment the Pope condemned the subscription the Catholic Irish raised £40,000. Ireland was under coercion. The peasants were suffering keenly. But no personal privations could make them forget the duty they owed to their leader and to their Church. Some one had blundered at the Vatican. Mr. Marum ingeniously demonstrated that the words *quibus positis*, in the final paragraph, involved the assumption that the Parnell subscription was being collected for the illegal purposes described in the earlier part of the letter. As this was not the case, the letter did not apply. It was necessary to give the Pope a lesson in such unmistakable loud fashion as is possible to loyal sons of the Church; so they doubled the Parnell Tribute as a hint to the Holy See, and hoped that in future the Pope would profit by the lesson. Unfortunately, he did not.

.&

CHAPTER XI.

THE PERSICO MISSION AND THE PLAN OF CAMPAIGN.

FOR the Pope's blunder about Mr. Parnell there was at
least one excuse. In 1883 the real nature of the service
which the Irish leader had done in weaning the Irish
from secret societies to rely upon Constitutional agitation was but imperfectly understood. The whole
English nation was hostile to him. He had but recently
come out of gaol, to which he had been committed by
a Liberal Ministry; and, more important than anything
else in the eyes of the Vatican, Cardinal M'Cabe, the
Archbishop of Dublin, was strongly opposed to the
Parnellite policy. There was, therefore, some excuse
for the Pope. But it would puzzle the most charitable
to discover any excuse for the extraordinary repetition
of the same blunder into which he fell five years later,
when he issued the Rescript condemning boycotting and
the Plan of Campaign. Why he did it no one at Rome
could say. All the interpretations believed in abroad
were categorically denied by Cardinal Rampolla. But
what the real explanation is no one even pretends to
know.

L

I was naturally anxious to find out the truth about
the matter, because I had been present at the Woodford
meeting when the Plan was first proclaimed, and I had
subsequently obtained from Archbishop Walsh, in 'an
interview at Dublin, his public sanction of the scheme.
But, notwithstanding all my efforts, I was unable to
ascertain who it was that put the Pope in motion, and
secured the decree of the Holy Office of which such use
was made. At one time I was assured that the case on
which the Holy Office had reported had been submitted
by the Bishop of Limerick, but just before I left Rome
that was authoritatively contradicted. The Pope,
according to the last version, submitted the case himself;
but under whose prompting he took this step no one
knows. Cardinal Rampolla authorised me to contradict
in the most categorical manner that the Pope had acted
under the pressure of the English Government. The
Marquis of Salisbury, the Duke of Norfolk, and Captain
Ross, of Bladensburg, were all invoked as conclusive
authorities as to the absence of any pressure from
England. Not, indeed, that there had been no representations from England. On the contrary, it was
frankly admitted that there had been any number of
suggestions, and even entreaties, that the Holy Father
would use his paternal authority to allay the agitation in
Ireland. But to all these he turned a deaf ear, refusing
to move hand or foot, until one fine day he suddenly
decided " all off his own bat," if the expressive vulgarism
may be pardoned, to send Monsignor Persico to report

on the position of affairs in the distracted island. He had cause for caution.

So far, then, as the great experiment of restoring the authority of the mediæval Popes had gone, it had not been a signal success, even in the Isle of the Saints, the closest Catholic preserve in the fold of the Church. In no country in the world are the laity as faithful and as zealous as in Ireland. Archbishop Croke was able to prove to the Pope that in his diocese 94 per cent. of the adult population regularly communicated. Unlike the rest of Western Europe, the democratic movement in Ireland flows in Catholic channels. The bishops are the leaders of the people, the priests the tribunes of their flocks. Yet, the moment the Pope ventured to stray beyond the innocuous region of pious commonplace, he was sharply told that " the paternal mind of the Holy Father, watchful as it ever was for the good of Ireland, had been greatly misled;" and his own bishops in their pastorals did not hesitate to warn him "how easy it would be to persuade a jealous and credulous race like the Irish that the Pope had acted on erroneous, prejudiced, and one-sided information." The Irish are never slow to appeal *de Papa male informato ad melius informandum.* All this was not encouraging. But Leo the Thirteenth is not a man who is easily dismayed; and —whether on the solicitation of the Duke of Norfolk, as the Irish believe, or entirely on his own initiative, who shall say?—he once more addressed himself to the question whether, as supreme pastor of the faithful, he could not take a more effective share in the guidance and governance of the Irish people.

The story of the origin of the Persico mission, as told in the *Contemporary Review*, was contradicted so flatly by Cardinal Rampolla as to the influence of English diplomacy upon the Holy See, that I should not have reproduced it here if there had been any other hypothesis to account for the untoward action of the Pope.

"The Persico mission originated in the attempt made by the English Government to enlist the authority of the Holy See on the side of 'law and order' in Ireland. A very interesting chapter may some day be written concerning the visits paid by the Irish bishops to Rome before this date; but this need not be dwelt upon now. Suffice it to say, that although the Pope was decidedly uneasy, owing to the representations of the English Catholics, who through Cardinal Howard and Monsignor Stonor had always easy confidential means of access to his ear, he consoled himself by reflecting upon the confidence of Archbishop Walsh, the proved fidelity of the Irish episcopate, and the fact that Cardinal Manning by no means shared the alarm of the English Catholics. But after the failure of Sir Michael Hicks-Beach's well-meant attempt to govern without coercion, by putting 'pressure within the law' upon the landlords who refused to make the necessary reductions of rent, a concerted effort was made to secure the services of the Pope as Unionist Emergency Man in Ireland. After a good deal of secret intrigue, upon which it may be necessary hereafter to shed more light than would be at present desirable, very strong pressure was brought to bear upon the Pope. Lord Salisbury had now fairly entered upon his policy of coercion, and the opposition of the Irish priests and bishops was the chief obstacle which baffled his efforts to reach his goal. It was hinted not obscurely that as Job did not serve God for naught, so the English Government would handsomely requite the Holy See for any services it might reader in muzzling the Irish priests. It is obvious that any English Government has many opportunities for doing a friendly turn to the Pope. The Empire of Britain stretches over all the continents, and its shores are washed by all the seas. No other world dominion confronts the policy of Rome at so many points. Even leaving Ireland apart, the State which includes within its borders the Catholic *habitans* of Quebec, and in whose colonies See after See of the Church has been established within the lifetime of this generation, is a power with which it is important to be on good terms. Ever since the great convulsion of the sixteenth century, the two great world dominions of Rome and of Britain, the Empire of the Confessional and the Empire of the Sea, had confronted each other, either in open hostility or in silent antagonism. It was hinted to Leo the Thirteenth that, if he were disposed to do his part, the English Government was willing to abandon the policy of the cold shoulder, and enter into more or less intimate diplomatic relations with the Holy See.

"It is not surprising that the Pope lent a willing ear to those faithful Catholics who implored him to seize an opportunity so unprecedented for bringing the Holy See into accord with the British Empire by accepting Lord Salisbury's overtures. Nothing seemed more natural to him than that he should endeavour to co-operate with the representatives of law and order. Himself the greatest of all authorities, he sympathised naturally with the authorities of Dublin Castle, and he had, on four previous occasions, made more or less feeble and ineffective efforts to restrain the priesthood in Ireland from participating in a revolutionary agitation, which, in his opinion, violated the moral law. The Holy Father was somewhat shy, but the bait was tempting. There was no question at first of securing the appointment of a Nuncio at the Court of St. James's, where none had been received for three hundred years; but much less than that would bring him perceptibly nearer to the goal of the temporal power. Mr. Gladstone, who has never purged himself from the offence of being the author of 'Vaticanism,' was known to be bitterly hostile to establishing diplomatic relations with the Vatican. Diplomatic relations only exist between temporal governments. Diplomacy is the intercourse of States. The Pope has no temporal authority. The

Papal States no longer exist. How then can a representative be accredited to the Vatican without implying the existence of some shadowy temporal sovereignty in the Pope, which cannot co-exist with the integrity of the Italian kingdom? So reasoned the Liberal leader, and it was clear nothing could be obtained from him. The bait was all the more tempting because the Pope knew that he could count upon no sympathy in his projects from Cardinal Manning. The Cardinal-Archbishop has never disguised his opinion that the appointment of a Nuncio would be disastrous to the best interests of the Church. The Pope, however, pre-occupied in the cherished dream of regaining temporal sovereignty in Rome, held those scruples in light esteem, and, after some coyness, decided that the opportunity was too good to be lost. It was, however, necessary to proceed with caution. The memory of the smart rebuke given to the Holy See by the doubling of the popular subscription to Mr. Parnell, as soon as it was known that the Pope had condemned it, naturally made the Holy Father chary of courting such another reminder of the fact that the Catholics of Ireland were still of the opinion of O'Connell, who said that while they took their religion from Rome, they would as soon take their politics from Stamboul.

" The Pope, therefore, decided to make a cautious move, and one to which no exception could be taken even by the most sensitive Irishman. Perplexed by conflicting representations, and grieved at the exacerbation of feeling consequent upon the introduction of the Coercion Bill, what was more natural than that he should despatch a special mission charged with the duty of personally investigating on the spot the facts of the case? So it was announced, with considerable flourish of trumpets, that Monsignor Persico was appointed as a Special Commissioner for the Holy See, to proceed to Ireland to inquire into and report upon the questions in dispute between the Irish and their rulers."

In view of the declarations of the Cardinal Secretary of State, we must assume that the Pope, although much pressed to take action in Ireland by the English Government, did not act in consequence of that pressure, and

that his action in sending Monsignor Persico was
entirely spontaneous on his part, and had no relation
whatever to the representations which had preceded it.

The selection which the Pope had made of his Envoy
has not been unwise—if an Italian had to be sent.
Monsignor Persico is one of the few Italian Monsignori
who can speak English. He was a Capuchin friar, who
held the titular Archbishopric of Damietta, and who had
been employed on many delicate diplomatic missions by
the Holy See in India, in Portugal, in Canada, and in
South Carolina. His career illustrates at once the cosmopolitan nature of the Church and the immense range
of its activities. Excepting the British Empire, there is
nothing like it in the world. Most of Monsignor Persico's life had been spent under the shadow of the
British flag. He had acted as Catholic chaplain to the
British troops in India; had founded and directed a
Catholic College at Darjeeling; and when the fabric of
our Empire was temporarily submerged by the Mutiny,
he was imprisoned by the Sepoys in the fortress of Agra.
After his release, he collected funds in Europe to repair
the ruin wrought in Catholic edifices by the Mutiny,
after which he became one of the most trusted Envoys
of the Holy See. Thirty years ago he came to London
on a special mission, connected with the interests of the
Church, the memory of which is faint and dim. In
1863 he was despatched to America, to endeavour to
allay the popular excitement that prevailed among the
Catholics of South Carolina at the close of the war. He

took part in the Council of the Vatican, after which he was sent on a mission to India, where he presided over the establishment of the hierarchy.   After this little was heard of him outside the Roman world until his selection as Papal Envoy to Ireland, in June, 1888.

Monsignor Persico commanded the confidence of the Pope, who selects as his favourites those who have rendered signal service to the Church.   He was perfectly at home in English, of which his Holiness does not understand one word.   He had performed many diplomatic missions with success.   What was more natural than that at this juncture the Pope should despatch him to Ireland to see what could be done?   The fact that Monsignor Persico was not fitted personally to command the confidence of the Irish people does not seem to have occurred to the mind of the Pope.   Such, however, was unfortunately the fact.   There are antipathies of race which no amount of logic or of grace can overcome, and the Irish, from prelate to peasant, did not take kindly to the Italian friar.   In personal appearance the Envoy is not unlike an Italian peasant, somewhat stout, with a straggling grey beard, sly, half-shut eyes, and a certain oily suavity which filled the Irish with distrust.   "I would not trust him further than I could throw him," said one Irish member; and it is an open secret that at least one Irish Archbishop regarded him from the first with unconcealed distrust.   As representative of the Pope, he was everywhere received with enthusiastic demonstrations of respect;

but Monsignor Persico did not personally inspire the Irish hierarchy with confidence.

Strict instructions were given to Monsignor Persico to avoid any appearance of being in connivance with the English Government. Monsignor Persico was hurried to Dublin without being allowed to make any stay in London, and no intimation whatever was sent to the English Government of the object of his mission. By way of further keeping up the semblance of impartiality, Monsignor Gualdi was attached to the mission as Persico's secretary. Monsignor Gualdi, although an Italian like his chief, had enjoyed the advantage of having worked for many years among the Irish Catholics in London under the eye of Cardinal Manning. He understood Ireland, and was in such notorious sympathy with the popular aspirations, that his selection as secretary was regarded as proof positive that the Persico mission was by no means intended to cover the muzzling of the clergy. Monsignor Gualdi accepted his mission in good faith. To quote his own simple words, spoken in Dublin immediately after his arrival, he believed that "the Holy Father wants to learn the condition of the country, just as if he were seeing it with his own eyes. He wants to do good to Ireland. He wants to be able to speak from facts collected on the spot. He could not, of course, come over himself, and so he sent us." Such, at least, was the honest conviction of this honest priest. When events proved how much he had been misled, and Monsignor Persico found it necessary to disembarrass himself of the assistance of a secretary who could not be bent to the service of the English Government, the good priest took it so much to heart that he took to his bed and died, chiefly, it is asserted in Rome, from a broken heart.

Monsignor Gualdi was from the first not in the confidence of the Italian camarilla, from which Monsignor Persico drew his instructions. He thought, for instance, that the Papal Envoy, after making a comprehensive study of the Irish question, would return to Rome and report to the Holy Father. That, however, was not the intention of the Pope. Monsignor Persico's mission was intended to be permanent. He was forbidden to return to Rome even when, like a true Italian, he pined for the blue sky, and fretted himself sick at the horror of wintering in these islands of the Northern Seas. Whether or not it was believed possible to develop the Papal mission into a regular Nunciature is buried in obscurity. What is known is that Monsignor Persico had positive orders to remain. If his health suffered in Ireland, he might be permitted to winter in England or Scotland, but outside of the three kingdoms he was not allowed to move. He might possibly have been here to this day but for the storm occasioned by the Rescript condemning the Plan of Campaign. But this is anticipating.

When Monsignor Persico first went to Ireland he kept up appearances. He went direct to Archbishop Walsh, the eulogist of the Plan of Campaign, and for a time all went well. The archbishops and

bishops were loud in their protestations of confidence
in the sympathy of the Holy See for Ireland. But,
after a time, a change came over the spirit of their
dream. Monsignor Persico began to inspire distrust.
He oscillated between the dinner-tables of landlords
and the palaces of the bishops. He was on good
terms with men engaged in administering an Act which
the hierarchy, with almost unanimous voice, had branded
as tyrannical and unjust. He certainly took no pains to
establish confidential relations with the leaders of the
popular party. When Monsignor Persico left Dublin to
meet the other Bishops in succession, he first went
south—not to the Archbishop of Cashel, or to any of the
Bishops of the Southern Ecclesiastical province, but to
Lord Emly, at whose house he stayed on a visit for some
days. In going there, and in returning to Dublin, he
passed by Thurles. This, the first indication of supposed
unfriendly feeling, caused intense indignation, especially
in the South of Ireland. During his stay in Ireland,
generally he went on visits to the houses of landlords like
the Hon. Villiers Stuart, Lord Bantry, Count de la Poer,
etc., etc. On the other hand, he declined an invitation
to meet Mr. T. D. Sullivan, M.P., the Mayor of Dublin,
who requested permission to invite him to dine at the
Mansion House. Thus suspicion deepened into distrust,
and distrust soon developed into a rooted conviction that
the sly Italian was playing them false. What he wrote to
Rome has never been published. It is a secret of the
Vatican. But, judging from common rumour, he con-

structed his reports on the principle of sitting on the fence. The Irish had grievances, but they compromised their cause with violence. The English Government was too severe, but some of the priests were too keen politicians. Home Rule was a just demand with modifications, but the Plan of Campaign involved a breach of contract. All that summer the diplomatic dodgery went on, Monsignor Persico writing letters to the Vatican, and the Irish popular distrust of Persico deepening into detestation. But Monsignor Persico, not content with writing private representations to the Pope, attempted to do a little "pacification" off his own bat. Being in confidential relations with the authorities, they apprised him from time to time when they intended imprisoning a priest. He then communicated with the bishop, who, through his vicar-general, put the screw upon the priest to induce him to act with the utmost caution and moderation, and, above all, not to do anything that might bring him under the lash of the Coercion Act. Perhaps nothing could be more natural, but to the Irish mind nothing could be more detestable than the Italian emissary of the Vicegerent of God making himself the cat's-paw and the go-between of the English oppressors. So the summer passed, and when the winter came Monsignor Persico drew up his report, and repaired to Bournemouth to await the return of spring, when he was once more to cross the Irish Sea.

Now here again I must quote the narrative in the *Contemporary Review*, with the proviso that Cardinal

Rampolla denies utterly the insinuation that the Pope's action was in any way prompted by the Duke of Norfolk :—

"While Monsignor Persico was preparing the ground in Ireland, his allies had not been idle. The Jubilee of Her Majesty had afforded an opportunity for an interchange of courtesies between the Vatican and St. James's, which it was determined to exploit to the uttermost. The Pope had sent a special envoy to congratulate the Queen. What more natural and fitting than that Her Majesty's Ministers should send a special envoy to the Pope to return his compliments, and to see whether, at the same time, anything could be done to bring about those closer and more intimate relations upon which the Pope had set his heart? The motive of Persico's mission was pretty well understood at the Foreign Office, and it was deemed advisable that a serious effort should be made to bring matters to a head, and commit the Pope to a policy of repression in Ireland. It was under these circumstances and with such hopes that the mission of the Duke of Norfolk was decided on.

"The Duke, who in England is a nonentity, is regarded at Rome with the respect due to a great noble who has preserved, in the midst of temptation, an unshaken loyalty to the Holy See. One Howard sat in the Sacred College, and the ducal head of the family had always been a welcome visitor at the Vatican. In the Councils of the Church, personal piety weighs for more than intellectual capacity, and the deficiencies of the Duke in one direction were more than compensated in another. All things considered, it would probably have been difficult to find a more acceptable go-between than the Duke. His task was comparatively simple. It is understood that he had to intimate, in more or less guarded phrase, that Her Majesty's Ministers were not indisposed to do a little business with the Holy See on the principle of *Do ut des.* If the Pope could see his way to use his moral influence to restrain the Irish bishops and clergy within the limits marked out by the English Government, then, perhaps, the English Government might see their way to meet the cherished aspirations of the Holy See for the re-establishment of direct diplomatic relations between the Vatican and the

Court at St. James's. The Liberal Government had for some time maintained, at a considerable economy of truth, a sort of unofficial representative at the Vatican in the person of Sir George Errington, and it was difficult to see what insuperable objection there could be to the accrediting of a British envoy on a regular footing. The Duke, it is believed, was further in a position to intimate that, besides the re-establishment of diplomatic relations, something might be done in the shape of a substantial subsidy and Government patronage for Catholic education in Ireland."

Whatever the cause, the Pope suddenly took action and sent down to the Holy Office, or, in other words, to the Inquisition, a case of conscience, asking them whether it was permissible to use the Plan of Campaign and boycotting. Of course, everything depends in such a reference upon the terms of the question, and the meaning attached to phrases employed. It is perfectly open to any Catholic to submit a case of conscience to the Holy Office, and the decision is given upon the case as he puts it. He may state the case incorrectly. That is not the concern of the Holy Office. They adjudicate solely upon that which is submitted. Their decision is limited to the mere case as submitted, and yet no precautions have ever been taken to secure, when judgment is pronounced, that it should be accompanied by the statement on which the decision was arrived at. A decree of condemnation may be obtained against a practice or a society by suppressing the vital fact which, even in the opinion of the Holy Office, would render the practice and the society quite lawful. The mischief arises in applying a censure obtained by a reference limited to one possibly misleading statement of facts to

a whole series of facts, with which it may have only had
the name in common. In order to understand what is
the value of the decision of the Inquisition about boycotting and the Plan of Campaign, it is necessary to
know how these Irish technicalities were translated, so as
to bring them before the Italian mind. But no information of that kind has ever been disclosed.

No one has ever explained why the Pope was in such a
monstrous hurry to send the matter before the Inquisition.
It was eighteen months after the Plan of Campaign had
been promulgated. Every consideration of duty and of
expediency counselled delay. Monsignor Persico, who
had been sent to Ireland on a special mission to enable
the Holy Father to see things with his own eyes, had not
reported. To ordinary mundane intelligence, it seems
somewhat absurd to despatch a special commissioner to
report upon the facts of a complex situation, and then to
proceed to deliver judgment before you have had time
to read your commissioner's report. A saving sense of
humour would have saved the Pope from such a blunder.
But, unfortunately, the very excellence of the motives of
the Pope, and his own strong sense of his supreme and
divine position, seem to make him feel that he may
without danger emancipate himself from the conditions
which other men impose upon themselves as security
against hasty and uninformed judgment. Monsignor
Persico had written many letters, even if he had not
drafted his final report. So Leo the Thirteenth set himself to deliver judgment.

It is interesting to note how, under such circumstances, the Supreme Court of Christendom addresses itself to the consideration of the case before it. The organisation of the Holy See is admitted universally to be such a masterpiece of human wisdom, that the faithful may be excused for seeing in it the inspiration of Heaven. Unfortunately, in the present instance, its deliberations can hardly be said to be worthy of imitation. To begin with, an Italian, pre-occupied with the aspiration for regaining sovereignty in Rome, decides to adjudicate upon one of the most difficult questions concerning the life of a nation whose existence has been little better than one long martyrdom at the hands of the English. Having so decided, the Pope, who has never been in Ireland, and who is incapable of speaking even one word of the language of the people, whose instincts are those of an authoritative ruler of a centralised organisation, the mainstay of governments and the bulwark of conservatism and order, sends down to the Congregation of the Inquisition, and demands a discussion on a case of conscience. A committee is then constituted, composed either exclusively, or all but exclusively, of Italians, who have never been in Ireland, and who are entirely out of touch with the solid realities of the situation, and to this committee the subject is referred for consideration. That committee, after some more or less general discussion, according to the wont of such bodies, appoints one of its members, who like every one else is an Italian, to draw up a draft report, which, after some further discussion, is finally approved and sent on to the Pope.

The Pope then considers what should be done with it. It might naturally be supposed, before he did anything with it, he would consult first Monsignor Persico, his trusted Envoy, and then Archbishop Walsh, who was at the time in Rome, waiting to explain to the Holy See all about the Plan of Campaign. Unfortunately, the Pope consulted neither the one nor the other.) Yet the Archbishop of Dublin had publicly approved the morality of the Plan of Campaign, which the Pope was now about to condemn. Archbishop Walsh, eighteen months before, had returned the following answers to my question whether "such a scandalous outrage on the principles of common honesty," as it was styled by every one, did not scandalise him :—

A. Well, I confess that at first I was a little startled at it. I was not only startled but grieved. I had never yet had cause to express my dissent from any portion of the programme of the present national movement. Notwithstanding all my sympathy with the movement, the adoption in this diocese of any unjust or immoral means for the furtherance of its object would, of course, put upon me the painful duty of publishing an episcopal condemnation of it. We Catholics, as you know, cannot act on the principle, rather fashionable, I am sorry to say, nowadays, that "the end justifies the means." So, apprehending that the "Plan of Campaign" might at any moment be brought into requisition in this diocese of Dublin, I was grieved to think, as I did think for the moment, that it might perhaps prove inconsistent with my duty as Bishop of the diocese to abstain from a condemnation of it. But when I looked into the matter carefully, as it was, of course, my

M

duty to do, my anxiety was relieved. On closer inspection, the difficulties that had at first embarrassed me practically disappeared. . . : This is how I would state my view of the case. It is admitted on all hands that practically all over Ireland reductions, and large reductions, are to be made in the rents, even in the judicial rents. The question is as to the amount of those reductions. Whatever inconvenience there may be in having that grave question decided by the tenants, I must maintain that there is just the same inconvenience—indeed, I see in one way a much greater inconvenience—in having it decided by the landlords. The landlord, like the tenant, is now merely "one of the two contracting parties," neither more nor less.

It is only fair, however, both to the Pope and to the Archbishop, to remember that the approval of the latter and the condemnation of the former were pronounced under altogether different circumstances. When the Archbishop had blessed the Plan of Campaign, the Government had refused to allow the creation of any legal means (1) for defining the relative proportion of the property belonging to landlord and tenant in the case of 120,000 leaseholders in Ireland, and (2) for fixing what was the extent of the reduction which undoubtedly ought to be made in the judicial rents. The Archbishop, being a practical man on the spot, seeing that some one must decide, and that Parliament had refused to supply a legal remedy, declared that the tenants had as good a right as the landlords to fix on what conditions they should be allowed to continue in occupation of their own property. Thanks largely to his courage and resolution, there was sufficient pressure brought to bear upon the Government to induce them in

the following year to provide legal means for deter-
mining the conditions of tenancy. This entirely altered
the situation. Had the Land Act of 1887 been passed
in 1886, the Archbishop would never have approved the
Plan of Campaign.

The Papal condemnation of the Plan was not issued
till nearly midsummer, 1888. But as early as October,
1887, Archbishop Walsh, in the course of an interview
on the case of the Coolgreaney tenants, who alone in his
diocese had adopted the Plan, explicitly declared that it
was the duty of all to adhere to the legal standard set up
by Parliament. At Coolgreaney the reductions claimed
by the Campaigners were less than those that would
have been awarded by the Court. Unfortunately, the
difficulties that arise when once peace has been broken
prevented the acceptance of the Archbishop's counsel.
He might have succeeded if he had not been paralysed
by the presence of Monsignor Persico. But for the evil
influence of this Italian emissary, the Archbishop might
have settled the few outstanding difficulties left over by
the Plan. But he dared not speak as strongly or act
as vigorously as he would otherwise have done, as his
action, in that case, would have infallibly been misinterpreted. The Irish would have believed that he acted, not
of his own judgment, but under pressure from Monsignor
Persico. That would have been fatal, not only for the
prospects of immediate settlement, but for the influence
of the Archbishop on all other questions.

Speaking with the wisdom that comes after the event,

it is no doubt deeply to be deplored that an opportunity was not given for a consideration of the whole case in Ireland. If a consultation had come off, such as Archbishop Walsh could have brought about but for the Papal Envoy's presence, all difficulties might have been avoided.

Owing, however, to the fact that there is no Irish Cardinal with right of access to the Pope, none of these considerations, known as they are to any one who was on the spot at the time, could be represented to the Vatican. Hence the Pope, by issuing his sweeping condemnation of the Plan of Campaign, occasioned needless scandal through sheer lack of information. If he had but discriminated between the Plan in 1886, before the law was altered, and the Plan in 1888, after the Land Act of 1887 had provided legal means for reducing rents, he would have avoided even an apparent conflict of opinion between the Archbishop of Dublin and the Bishop of Rome. Of course, on all questions as to the unlawfulness of resisting coercion by other than legal and constitutional means there could not be, even in appearance, any difference of opinion between Archbishop Walsh and the Holy Office. When the Plan was started, it was laid down that the tactics were to be strictly confined within the limits allowed by the law. In practice this restriction was sometimes forgotten.

Whatever view may be taken of the matter, it was, according to ordinary mundane notions of fair play, the first and most obvious duty of the Pope to accord Archbishop Walsh a full and patient hearing.

Nothing startled and grieved me more when I was in Rome than to hear that the Pope did no such thing. Archbishop Walsh was months in Rome waiting for a hearing. He never got it until after the decree was published.

The Pope treated Monsignor Persico almost as cavalierly. At present Monsignor Persico has to bear the brunt of the blame, for the Church never hesitates to sacrifice its instruments in order to protect its head. But, in the interests of truth it is necessary to say quite clearly that it is the Pope and not Monsignor Persico who must bear the blame for the recent peril into which the Church has been plunged in Ireland. Monsignor Persico's lips are closed for the present, and he cannot make any reply to the hurricane of abuse with which he has been overwhelmed. Should the time come when he can be heard in his own defence, the world and the Church will be surprised indeed.

It is therefore all the more incumbent upon those who know the facts as they are known in Rome to do an act of tardy justice to Monsignor Persico, who, so far from deserving the censure so freely heaped upon him, may fairly claim to have seen the rock upon which the Holy Father steered, and to have urged him, unfortunately in vain, to adopt an altogether different course to that which he persisted in pursuing.

This is a very grave statement, which is not made without positive knowledge at first hand of the facts. In justice to Monsignor Persico, it should be known in Ireland—

1. That so far from the Rescript having been drawn up in accordance with his recommendations, there were few men in all Ireland more astonished, and, it may be added, dismayed, than was Monsignor Persico on the receipt of that fateful document. He was not consulted about it while it was in process of elaboration; he did not recommend that it should be issued; and the first intimation which he received that such a momentous step was to be taken was his receipt, in common with the Irish bishops, of the text of the Rescript.

2. That not only did Monsignor Persico not advise the publication of the Rescript, but in his reports, which he forwarded to the Vatican for the information of the Holy Father, he expressly and urgently deprecated any such precipitance, and implored the Pope to do nothing whatever in Ireland until he had summoned the Archbishops and one Bishop from every province in Ireland to Rome, and had gone into all the questions of fact and of principle with those who were most competent to advise.

3. That when the Pope, in his letter of June 24, 1888, defending his Rescript, told the Irish Bishops that his sources of information were trustworthy, and that he could not be justly accused of having given judgment in a case with which he was insufficiently acquainted, because he had sent Monsignor Persico "with the commission to use the greatest diligence in ascertaining the truth and to make a faithful report to us," he seems to have implied that his Rescript was based upon the

report of Monsignor Persico. Although the Pope may have read the earlier letters of his Envoy, the contrast between Monsignor Persico's final advice and the Pope's action seems to indicate that his *Relazione* had not even been perused by the Pope before he launched the Rescript which created so much heart-burning in Ireland.

4. That Monsignor Persico, so far from desiring to make the Church the tool of the English Government, declared throughout that it was fatal to the influence of the Holy See in Ireland that the Pope's action should be in any way suspected to be prompted by England. He had considerable experience in negotiating with Catholic Governments, and his conviction was very strong that the expectations of the Pope of gain from diplomatic relations with England were mistaken. They would not strengthen, and they might easily weaken, the authority of the Church. The hierarchy of Ireland, he maintained, were the true and proper channels through whom all communications should take place between the Pope and the Irish people.

Nevertheless, without waiting to read Monsignor Persico's *Relazione*, and without condescending to take any note of his advice, the Rescript was drawn up and despatched to the Propaganda for transmission to the Irish bishops.

When I was at the Propaganda, I was assured that it had not been the intention of the Pope to have the "Rescript" published at all. It was confidentially transmitted to the bishops, who were to act on it as of their own motive. This was spoiled by an indiscretion. Monsignor Agliardi, since "promoted" to be Nuncio at Munich, was an Italian, who, when on a mission in India, had been captivated by the smiling suavity of the Viceroy. He learned the nature of the " Rescript," and communicated the fact of its approaching despatch to the Roman correspondent of the *Daily Chronicle*. This gentleman telegraphed it to London, from whence it was telegraphed back by the Stefani Agency, to the infinite dismay of the Propaganda and the justifiable wrath of Archbishop Walsh. The gross breach of all etiquette, in allowing a Papal Rescript to become known to the press before it reached the bishops to whom it was addressed, shocked the Pope, and, according to Roman report, Archbishop Walsh had the sympathy of the Pope in his protest against Monsignor Agliardi's indiscretion.

The decree, however, was issued. In condemning boycotting and the Plan of Campaign, it assumed as a 'postulate the existence of free contract between landlords and tenants in Ireland. Assuming that to exist which did not exist, its censure was nothing more than a shot fired in the air. *Bos locutus est*, and to as little purpose and with as little intelligence as is common to the species. It was a *brutum fulmen*, which irritated without overawing, and alarmed without convincing those to whom it was addressed.

Its text was as follows :—

"On several occasions the Apostolic See has given to the

people of Ireland (whom it has always regarded with special benevolence) suitable admonitions and advice, when circumstances required, as to how they might defend their rights without injury to justice or the public peace. Our Holy Father, Leo XIII., fearing lest in that species of war that has been introduced amongst the Irish people into the contests between landlords and tenants, and which is commonly called the Plan of Campaign, and in that kind of social interdict called boycotting from the same contests, true sense of justice and charity might be perverted, ordered the Supreme Congregation of the Inquisition to subject the matter to serious and careful examination. Hence the following question was proposed to their Eminences the Cardinals of that Congregation :—

"Is it permissible, in the disputes between landowners and tenants in Ireland, to use the means known as the Plan of Campaign and boycotting?

"After long and mature deliberation, their Eminences unanimously answered in the negative, and the decision was confirmed by the Holy Father on Wednesday, the 18th of the present month.

"The justice of this decision will be readily seen by any one who applies his mind to consider that a rent agreed on by mutual consent cannot, without violation of a contract, be diminished at the mere will of the tenant, especially when there are tribunals appointed for settling such controversies, and reducing unjust rents within the bounds of equity, after taking into account the causes which diminish the value of land. Neither can it be considered permissible that rents be extorted from tenants and deposited in the hands of unknown persons to the detriment of the landowners. Finally, it is contrary to justice and charity to persecute by a social interdict those who are satisfied to pay the rents they agree to, or those who, in the exercise of their right, take vacant farms.

"It will therefore be your Lordship's duty, prudently, but effectually, to advise and exhort the clergy and the laity not to transgress the bounds of Christian charity and justice whilst they are striving for a remedy for their distressed condition.

(Signed) "R. CARDINAL MONACO.

"Rome, April 20, 1888."

In Ireland the "Rescript" was received with an angry outburst of indignation, which found a convenient whipping-boy in the Papal Envoy. Ever since the appearance of that sinister and ill-omened document, Monsignor Persico has been one of the most detested of living men. "And who is that?" said a recent distinguished visitor to Rome, as in the midst of a throng of ecclesiastics he saw a dignitary clad in the brown garb of a Capuchin friar. "Oh," said his cicerone, "that is Monsignor Persico." "The saints preserve us!" was the reply; and the speaker, with horror and alarm on his features, crossed himself as diligently as if the shadow of the Evil One had fallen across his path. So vehement was the chorus of denunciation, that Monsignor Persico was alarmed for his own safety. Incredible as it may appear to those who know how foreign such a crime is to the Catholic Irish, it is actually the fact that he believed and said that his life was in danger. It was with a feeling of profound relief that he received permission to return to Rome, where he is now looking after the Copts, and discharging the other duties which belong to the Secretariat of the Oriental rites to which he was promoted some months after his return.

Never for many years has there been such a commotion as was excited by the "Rescript." The bishops of Ireland, with one exception, omitted to publish it to their flocks. Monsignor Mocenni, the Under State Secretary, an Italian who had much experience of Vienna, but who regards Ireland from the con-

ventional standpoint of ecclesiastical discipline, was
scandalised. "They are revolutionaries," he exclaimed;
"all revolutionaries—the whole people,—how dare they
refuse to publish the 'Rescript' in Ireland?" They did
dare, and after a while they were able to convince the
Holy Father that they were wiser in their disobedience
than he was in his "Rescript." The Pope was sincerely
alarmed by the storm which he had excited. All
Ireland seemed to be up in arms, and the most faithful
Catholics were those who took the lead in denouncing
the "Rescript."

The Bishop of Limerick, of course, was prompt to
avail himself of the Papal cover for his own opinions.
Boycotting and the Plan of Campaign, he told his clergy,
as they actually existed in Ireland, stood condemned as
violations of the moral law, of charity and justice. This
was no longer a matter of opinion: it was now a settled
and a certain law of the Catholic Church, which all the
faithful of the diocese were bound to take from him
their Bishop, that this practice was sinful, and more
sinful, as being against faith, to deny or impugn under
any pretext the right of the Pope to condemn it. . . .
The Pope has a divine and inalienable right to interfere
in all questions in which faith and morals are concerned,
and so forth.

The Pope himself, irritated at the protests in Ireland, so far forgot the dates and the facts as to say
in a letter to the Irish Bishops that he had investi-
gated the matter in personal interview with them-

selves.   How many Irish Bishops were personally interviewed by the Pope on the subject of the Plan of
Campaign?   He told them that "they must take all
necessary steps so that no room be left for doubt as to
the force of the decree.   Let it be understood by all
that the entire method of action whose employment we
have forbidden is forbidden as altogether unlawful."
Nevertheless, the Irish Bishops explained away the
"Rescript," and it has only been applied in one
solitary instance.   To add to the chagrin and dis-
appointment of the well-meaning but injudicious Pope,
the only voices raised in approval were those of
the habitual enemies of himself and his people, who
hardly cared to conceal the note of mockery and exultation with which they hailed the discomfiture of the
Irish Catholics.   To delight the enemies of the faith,
and to fill the faithful with confusion and dismay, was
not exactly the end which the Pope had set before
himself when, with unwise precipitance, he plunged into
the Irish bog.   Fortunately, he was wise enough and
bold enough to see his mistake, and to endeavour to
reverse it.   An apologetic explanation was published.
All negotiations with the Duke of Norfolk were abruptly
broken off.   The Duke suddenly returned to England
from Italy without having the audience which had been
arranged.   Monsignor Persico was recalled, and since
that date the Holy See has suspended all further
attempts to interfere in Irish affairs.

The formula under which this change of policy is

concealed is a decision that, before any fresh step is taken, the Irish and American Bishops, and, if possible, those of Australia also, shall be consulted—a resolution of vast and far-reaching significance.

The lesson which this story teaches as to the perils which encompass the Church when the Sovereign Pontiff, the successor of the Prince of the Apostles, and the Vicar upon earth of our Lord Himself, can thus set at defiance the ordinary rules of statesmanship, is, that it is not enough to have your head in the clouds : you must also have your feet firmly planted upon solid facts.

The Pope's ideal of embodying the voice of the Christian conscience is an admirable one; but it requires omniscience for its realisation. If he would essay to prescribe for the moral and spiritual ailments of mankind, the first condition is a careful diagnosis of the state of his patient. It does not do to send "a man of tried prudence and discretion" to report upon a case, and then to prescribe without reading his report. No amount of respect due to the holiness of his office, or the excellence of his intentions, can prevent the Pope from making grievous mistakes prejudicial to his own authority, if he ventures to pronounce judgment upon subjects which he does not fully understand, without taking the advice of those who are on the spot, and whose authority he is always exhorting the faithful to obey.

CHAPTER XII.

REFORM AND REDISTRIBUTION.

In the great church of the Gesù, where Ignatius Loyola lies enshrined in one of the most splendid temples reared by human devotion to the memory of its benefactors, two sculptured groups attract the eye of every visitor. One, to the right of the altar, beneath which rest the ashes of the saint, represents the Destruction of Paganism; the other, on the left, the Extirpation of Heresy. The destroying angels, full of savage energy, smite and spare not as they fall upon the enemies of the Church. Some day, perhaps not in the distant future, a new and stately temple will arise over the tomb of another saint, to whom has been reserved the glory of launching the thunderbolt of destruction against Pauperism and Prostitution, against Intemperance and Slavery. And before that shrine the whole human race will bow in a Catholicity wider than any that Rome has yet realised, in worship that is unmarred by the savage discords of sectarian strife.

Is it a vain dream that perchance this new Loyola,. who will found a Society of the Servants of Man, may arise within the pale of the Roman Church? Who that reflects upon the marvellous adaptabilities, the extraordinary genius, and the recuperative power of the Catholic Church can refuse to admit at least as a possibility that under the pressure of the stern facts of life— those grim schoolmasters of God—we may yet see even this evolution? If the Church addresses itself in earnest to the solution of the social question, who can say what may happen? At present, no doubt, the Church has got sadly out of gear. It has lost touch with the times. It has lagged behind in the march of progress. The mere suggestion that it may perhaps not altogether be a waste force in the sum of human endeavour is received with angry and incredulous scorn by the descendants of the men whom the Church civilised and placed in the van of human progress. But this estrangement may be but temporary. The genius of our time is opposed to relegating anything to the dust heap. The triumph of our civilisation is the utilisation of everything that exists. There is no waste in nature, and it is contrary to every scientific principle to suppose that mankind will fail to discover any means of utilising an institution as immense as the Catholic Church. No doubt there is much that has become obsolete. Churches, like trees, have need to shed their leaves. It is the law of growth. But if there be but vitality in the trunk, if the roots are anchored deep with living grasp in the heart of mother earth, the fall of the leaf is but the harbinger of coming spring. A good many old leaves are falling off the Catholic Church to-day, and more will fall before the spring arrives. But it is too close to the heart of the world for us to doubt but that the spring will surely come.

In all human institutions existing in the world at this hour, the German headquarters' staff probably represents most nearly the perfect flower of the organizing and directing intellect of man. For the defence of the Fatherland, encamped as it were in the very midst of possible enemies, every faculty of the German brain has been taxed to the uttermost. There is not a weak place on the frontier but measures have been devised for its protection, not a gap in the line of defence to which a competent force is not already told off to fill. Nor is there a single fencible man in all Germany who, on hearing the electric words, "Krieg. Mobil," does not know exactly where to go and what to do. There we have supreme intelligence directing forces animated by implicit obedience and confident loyalty with such success that, within ten days from the declaration of war, the whole mobilised force of the Empire could be launched as an irresistible thunderbolt into the heart of the enemy's country. What is wanted is something of the same intelligence to direct and the same unhesitating loyalty to obey in the vast field of humanitarian reform. At present the world, from the point of view of the reformer, presents a sad and sorry spectacle. In

the great campaign against the evils which afflict society,
every regiment fights for its own hand, without concert,
without communication. There is no Intelligence Department in the humanitarian movement. It is aimless,
fitful, inorganic. Instead of concentrating all their force
on the weakest point of the enemy's position, our troops
scatter their fire aimlessly all along the line, and occasionally blaze into each other's ranks, by way of protest
against a difference of regimentals. Imagine Germany
split up once more into the old multiplicity of kingships
and principalities, and with the headquarters' staff abolished, and you have, compared with the Germany of
to-day, the contrast in effective force which would exist
between the aimless and sporadic warfare that is waged
to-day by the humanitarian forces of the world and the
irresistible plan of campaign that might be organized if
mankind had some common centre for deliberation,
co-operation, and direction. I hope no one will do me
the injustice of imagining that I hanker after anything
approaching a system of drill-sergeant in any department
of human life, least of all in things moral, social, and
spiritual. But that which has been achieved by a
centralised despotism in military affairs may be accomplished by intelligent co-operation and voluntary association in the freer realm of humanitarian endeavour.
The question is, whether the Holy See, with its great
position and splendid traditions of human service, may
become the centre of organized human effort for the
amelioration of the lot of men, not by virtue of any

N

arbitrary authority, human or divine, but because it
may make itself the heart and the brain of collective
humanity.

It is not impossible. But certain conditions will have
to be complied with before it is possible, and the first of
these is that it must leave Rome. The evil traditions of
a centralised Empire based on force cling to the very
stones of the Imperial city. Authority is in the air of
the Vatican, and by a strange and providential dispensation, the place where the temptation to rely upon authority is strongest is the place where the possibility of
exerting even moral influence is the least. To me the
chief element of hope for the Catholic Church in our
time has been the destruction of the Temporal Power.
Whatever may have been its uses once, it had become
as the cerements of the grave round the living body of
the Church. Now the tomb has been opened, and
Lazarus has come forth. But, however beneficent the
change, it has created an aggravated and inflamed condition of mind on both sides, which is fatal to any
utilisation of the Holy See for secular service as long as
it remains in Rome. Every action of the Pope would
be misinterpreted. Every proposal he made would be
rejected. For it must never be forgotten that at the
present moment in all sad verity the Pope is far more
really a bishop *in partibus infidelium* than any of the
hierarchy in English-speaking lands. In no city in the
English-speaking world, not even in Belfast, where "To
hell with the Pope!" is the favourite watchword of the

corner boys of the Orange quarter, would the Pope be regarded with anything approaching the same rancorous hostility with which he is regarded by the majority of the active politicians in Rome. The first condition of the adaptation of the Papacy to the new era is that its chief must quit Rome. He will never do so of his own accord; but if Providence wills for the Holy See a wider mission than can be fulfilled at the Vatican, the reluctance of an individual to change his quarters will not count.

The second change that is equally indispensable, and which would naturally follow the transference of the Holy See from Rome to some place nearer the centre of the forces which are shaping the modern world, is what we in England would describe as a redistribution of seats. Never, until I was actually in Rome, did I realise the extent to which the Temporal Power had destroyed the very ideal of a Catholic Church. The whole administration of what was supposed to be the Cosmopolitan Church Universal had been degraded into a mere prefecture of a single city. Every office is stuffed with Italians. When I exclaimed against this Italianisation of the Church, I was asked how it could possibly be avoided. The Pope reigned in Rome. His subjects were Italians. He could not govern them by Frenchmen or Germans or, Englishmen. And thus the interests of the Church Universal were deliberately subordinated to the administrative necessities of a city not the size of Glasgow. Of course this might work so long as the business of the

Church outside Rome was solely theological. There are no nationalities on the other side of the grave. But the moment you attempt to make the Holy See a living centre of the actual forces of the modern world, you will have to make the administration as cosmopolitan as the area of its jurisdiction. The change will have to begin with the Pope, and go right down to the Minutante in the Congregations.

Cardinal Lavigerie was interviewed last month about the chances of his selection as the successor of Leo XIII. He laughed the idea to scorn. "The Italians," he said, "would never renounce the preponderance which had enabled them to monopolise the Holy See for the last hundred years. It is as absurd to talk of a French Pope as it is to dream of seizing the moon with one's teeth." That is not the sentiment which should exist in any institution really cosmopolitan and international. But it is inevitable that all the other nationalities should feel the same. The Italians exploit the whole Church. Nothing impressed me more when I came to look into the matter than the analogy there is between the Curia and the old unreformed House of Commons. There is just the same disproportion between the representatives and the represented. Gatton and Old Sarum have their full quota of members. Birmingham and Manchester are left out in the cold. At the beginning of the year, according to the official "Gerarchia," there were only 60 cardinals in the Sacred College. Of these 32 were Italians, while the remaining

28 red hats were distributed over all the rest of the world. Italy, which, when every anti-clerical is reckoned as a Catholic, does not contain more than one-eighth of the faithful, is thus allotted more than one-half of the seats in the Sacred College. Even this is a very inadequate representation of the case against the existing system. The Italian cardinals are on the spot. Of the others, the greater proportion are appointed as a kind of honorary distinction. They live in distant capitals, and their share as to the administration of the Curia is practically of the slightest. For instance, Cardinal Manning is in Westminster, Cardinal Newman in Birmingham, while Cardinal Howard has come home to die. Cardinal Moran is in Melbourne, and Cardinal Gibbons in Baltimore. Yet, if Dr. Gibbons had not been a cardinal, the Pope would have blundered as badly about the Knights of Labour as he did about the Plan of Campaign. Had Archbishop Walsh worn the red hat, we may rely upon it that the Pope would have escaped the pitfall of the Persico "Rescript." While the Italians have more than 50 per cent. of the College, they have more than 80 per cent. of the actual working staff. It is they who manage everything. What they lack in faith they make up in wire-pulling. All the spoils go to them. There is hardly a high administrative office in the patronage of the Holy See that is not given to an Italian. If they do not live for the Church, they at least live on it. The present Pope, who has the instincts of a statesman, has endeavoured to move in the direction of diminishing

the Italian preponderance at headquarters. When he came to the Pontifical throne, there were thirty-eight Italian cardinals against twenty-five non-Italians. At the beginning of the year the numbers were 32 to 28. Yet Leo XIII., during his eleven years' reign, has created 37 Italian cardinals and 21 non-Italian. It will require much more drastic reform than this to bring the headquarters' staff of the Church into correspondence with the forces which it is to direct. No one would, of course, propose to demand the rigorous application of a system of proportional representation to the College of Cardinals. But the general principle that the interests of unrepresented people are apt to be overlooked holds so far good in affairs ecclesiastical as well as in affairs political, that it may be worth while roughly to jot down, side by side, the number of red hats allotted the different nations, and the number that would be accorded to them if distribution went according to population. I take the figures from the "Atlas des Missions Catholiques" and the official "Gerarchia," merely premising that it is monstrously absurd to count all the freethinkers of France and Italy as Catholics, while excluding all the non-Catholic Christians in England and America. As, however, this absurdity strengthens the case in favour of the *status quo*, I let it pass without further comment.

THE CATHOLIC WORLD AND THE COLLEGE OF CARDINALS.

Country.	Catholics.	Cardinals.	Due Proportion.
France	36,400,000	7	10
Austria-Hungary	29,580,000	4	8
Italy	28,000,000	32	8
Spain ... —	16,870,000	4	4
Germany —	16,230,000	3	4
Belgium ...	5,500,000	—	2
Poland	4,500,000	1	1
Portugal —	4,300,000	2	1
Ireland ...	3,960,000	—	1
Great Britain ...	1,320,000	3	—
Other Countries	6,000,000	—	2
* America ...	51,000,000	2	15
Asia	9,000,000	—	3
† Africa	2,600,000	1	1
‡ Australia —	670,000	1	1
		—	—
		60	61

* Cardinal Moran (Irish). Cardinal Taschereau (French Canadian).
† Cardinal Lavigerie (French).
‡

The whole of Catholic South America is unrepresented in the Sacred College.   Even if we do not accept
Mr. Gladstone's principle, that the more distant places
have a right to more rather than less representation, this
neglect of South America is inexplicable. The representation of Germany and Austria is miserably inadequate.
Can the eccentric Hohenlohe and the worn-out veteran
Melchers be regarded as an adequate representation of
the race whose genius for organization dominates
Europe? We have no doubt more than our fair share,
but none of our cardinals reside in Rome.   But I have
said enough to show how utterly impossible it is for even

the Catholic nations to regard the Curia as in any sense
an adequate representation of their interests. If ever the
Pope is to be Commander-in-Chief of the Humanitarian
forces of the world, he will have to recruit his headquarters' staff more evenly from all the nations under his
control.

The Holy See is in another matter just about one
hundred years behind the times. The Pope is very
anxious to be in diplomatic relations with the Governments of the day. It is the fashion in some quarters to
attribute this solely to a desire on his part to secure
some shadowy foothold from which he might reascend
the throne of Temporal Power. That, no doubt, is one of
the motives actuating the Holy See; but it is not the
only one. At bottom the craving for Nuncios is based
upon a very natural and proper desire on the part of the
Holy Father to be in actual touch with the representatives
of the nations in the midst of whom the Church exists.
But what is not yet recognised at the Vatican is, that the
last hundred years have so totally shifted the real centre
of national vitality, that it is almost as absurd to seek to
get in touch with the nations by the machinery of
diplomacy as it would be to trust to semaphores to
transmit telegrams. While the Vatican is vainly sighing
for the establishment of direct diplomatic relations with
the Court of St. James's, it entirely neglects the simple
and obvious means of communication with the people
who dictate the policy of the Court which lies ready to
its hands. A Pope who recognised the part which the

press plays in the modern world could afford to laugh at
the archaic machinery of nunciatures. But so far from
recognising this, the Vatican is almost entirely without
any means of communication with the press of the
world. Newspaper correspondents will tell you in
despair that, after repeated attempts, they have abandoned all hope of ever obtaining any news from the
Vatican. Yet the Holy See is a perfect hive of news of
all descriptions, which arrives from all parts of the world.
and might be distributed all over the world, to the very
great advantage of the Holy See and of the public. But
there is no Correspondence Bureau at the headquarters
of the Church; there is not even the feeblest attempt on
the part of the Catholic Church to employ the machinery
which Prince Bismarck has found so invaluable for the
education and manipulation of the public press. The
officials at headquarters bitterly complain of the falsity
of most of the news sent from Rome. They have only
themselves to blame for it. If correspondents are compelled to make bricks without straw, it cannot be
wondered at if the results are unsatisfactory. It is true
that there are two newspapers, the *Osservatore Romano*
and the *Moniteur de Rome*, which are in a way the
organs of the Vatican; but they seldom publish news
until it has ceased to be news, and is blue mouldy from
age. Actuality is a word the meaning of which the
Vatican has still to learn. The Holy See claims to be
nearly two thousand years old, and with the years of
Methuselah it has acquired much of that antediluvian

patriarch's indifference to time.   The leisurely habits of
a clumsy Saurian of the Pliocene period are, however,
ridiculously out of place in the last quarter of the nineteenth century, when men talk by telephone, correspond
by telegraph, and read morning and evening all the news
of all the world for the previous twelve hours.   Of all
functionaries, he whom the Church most needs to-day is
a real live editor who would keep the Vatican and the
press in close electric touch all over the world.   He
would not cost as much as a single Nuncio, and he
would be worth more than them all.

This brings me to the next change, which seems
indispensable if the Holy See is to regain its lost position, and which could be adopted without any violence
being done either to faith, doctrine, or its ecclesiastical
organization.   The Pope is surrounded by a host of
Congregations, which constitute the departments or
committees of the Church.   There are the Congrega-
gations of the Propaganda, of the Index, of Indulgences
and Rites, and so forth without end.   There is no Congregation charged with the study of the Social Question.
It is time there were.   There is no need to suppress
any of the existing Congregations.   All that is necessary
is to add another, which would be to the whole industrial populations of Christendom what the Congregation
of the Propaganda is to the heathen world.   If the Pope
is not to stultify himself by dealing with benevolent
officiousness in matters upon which he is imperfectly
informed, and with which he is in no official relation,

the sooner he gets his Congregation of the Social Question the better. It will certainly not lack for business. If it is well manned and up to its work, it may make itself the headquarters of the new International, and exercise a beneficent influence on the emancipation of labour throughout Christendom. While its primary function would be to keep the Pope informed, it would be not less useful in stimulating every priest in the Church to regard the social amelioration of the condition of the people in the midst of whom he was living as one of the most important of his duties. The establishment of such a Congregation is the logical corollary of the Pope's promises to the French pilgrims. If it is not established, it will be understood that beyond the emission of philanthropic aspirations the Holy Father does not mean to go.

When that Congregation is established, an opportunity will be afforded for marking the appreciation by the Holy See of the altered position of women in the New Era. The Church which has exalted woman in the person of the Madonna, and has long set an example to the world in the career which it afforded to women in the establishment and control of great religious orders, can have no objection to recognise the necessity of admitting women to a position as consulters on the Committee which is to advise the Church on the social question. Of the four leading points in the Pope's social programme, one concerns woman exclusively, a second relates to the employment of her children, and the other two apply equally to both men and women. To have a Congregation of the Social Question from which women were excluded would be absurd. To admit them would be the most signal demonstration of the appreciation of the Holy See of the importance of woman's influence in the State in the altered circumstances of the modern world.

Another matter, in which there is room for a good deal of improvement, is the matter of languages. What the headquarters of the Church really needs is a perennial renewal of the gift of tongues, which startled Jerusalem on the Day of Pentecost. Failing miracle, even the Holy See must have recourse to science, and its headquarters' staff should be a little more polyglot than it is to-day. In older days Latin was the universal language of the Church—the *lingua franca* of mediæval civilisation. It has played its part; but the time is coming when it will be succeeded by another. That language will not be Volapuk, much less will it be French. The common speech of the New Era will be the tongue which Milton spoke and Shakespeare wrote.

In the readjustment of the machinery of the Church to the altered needs of the New Era, I have suggested nothing that in any way infringes upon the province of the supernatural. The sacred deposit of faith and doctrine I have scrupulously left intact. It is not with such matters that I have had to do in my visit here.

No devout Catholic can accuse me of the sin of Uzzah, who laid profane but helping hand on the Ark of the Covenant. Accepting the Holy See at its own valuation, I have simply endeavoured to point out what are some of the most obvious changes which seem to be dictated by prudence to enable the Church to attain its avowed ends. It will hardly be contended by any save the sceptics, who are full of scorn at the idea of any one treating the Catholic Church seriously, that the Divine guidance promised to the Church would be withheld if the postal address of the Pope did not happen to be at Rome. That would, indeed, be to degrade the Catholic faith to the level of the old pagan superstition, which believed that the Divine oracle could only be consulted in the Delphic cave.

It is true that "B. O. S.," the writer of the pamphlet on the Roman question which was handed to me on my first visit to the Vatican, does endeavour to develop the theory of the necessity for the Temporal Power into a kind of necessary corollary to the dogma of Infallibility. If his contention were sound, it would only tend to prove how indispensable for the Catholic Church is the existence of outsiders who are free to call attention to the mistakes of its head without being exposed to accusations of mutiny. As for the other point, the need for the redistribution of seats, not even the most arrogant Italian of them all can pretend that the eternal monopoly of all the offices of the Church by the compatriots of Victor Emmanuel and of Mazzini is essential to the preservation of the original deposit of faith.

There are many things in the Church in Rome calculated to excite the liveliest repugnance on the part, not merely of Protestants, but Catholics accustomed to the more sober and rational worship of other lands. General Ignatieff's unaffected indignation at the mingled irreverence and superstition which he met in many of the Roman churches was quite irrepressible. " I understand Luther now," he exclaimed. " If I were a Catholic, two days in Rome would make me a Protestant." No one, however, can accuse me in these letters of allowing any of my hereditary Puritanism to betray me into even an unsympathetic word. All that I ask is, that supernatural things should not be allowed to monopolise the exclusive attention of the good men and women who form the working force of the Catholic Church in all lands. There are other things in the world which demand attention not less urgently than the veneration of departed saints, or even than the execration of cremated heretics. What is wanted is a readjustment of perspective quite as much as a redistribution of seats.

A single illustration will suffice. This year has not been uneventful in the history of our race. The dawn of the New Era draws nigh. East and west, north and south, there is a stirring among the peoples. New ideas are in the air, and in the heart of the labouring man

there is growing a great hope that at last the travail of
the ages is about to bring forth a new and better social
order. From his palace-prison at the Vatican the Pope
can " tune all the pulpits " of Catholic Christendom, and
he has only to signify his will to cause anything he
pleases to be read aloud in the hearing of all the congregations of the faithful. What has be done this year?
He has pleaded for more prayers to St. Joseph, and be
has denounced the monument to Giordano Bruno. Can
it be said, even by the most devoted Catholic, that the
Holy Father by this means has made any serious attempt
to influence the living forces of our time?

Given all these changes—that is to say, the Holy See
removed from the Vatican to the freer atmosphere of
the Western world, the Curia and the *personnel* of the
administration brought approximately nearer to a pro-
portionate representation of the whole of the constituent
sections of the Catholic Church, a Congregation for social
questions established, on which women would have a right
to be consulted equally with men, a newspaper and correspondence bureau in full working order, and the progressive
substitution of English for Latin as the universal language of the Church,—given all these changes, or even
some tangible approach thereto, and the effective force
of the Holy See in the modern world would be im-
mensely increased. None of these changes is at variance with the faith, doctrine, and discipline of the
Church. These are merely readjustments, which would
enable the Church to adapt its somewhat antiquated

machinery to the ever-changing needs of the new time. If to all of these developments you add a young and energetic Pope, with an eye to see, an ear to hear, and sufficient faith in the heart of him to dare to put the Church to the crucial test of using it unhesitatingly as a weapon to smite every evil that afflicts the world, and as an instrument to help mankind to attain every aspiration after a higher and nobler life, we should cease to sigh after the glories of Gregory and the triumphs of Hildebrand in the splendour of the achievements of the new reign.

CHAPTER XIII

IS A HUMANISED PAPACY POSSIBLE?

IT is easy, no doubt, to make mincemeat of all my pious imaginings and charitable hopes concerning the possibility of a humanised Papacy by copious quotations from the Syllabus and the Encyclicals of various Popes, not excepting those of Leo XIII. If any one imagines that he thereby scores a point against his antagonist, well and good. But as I have never maintained that the Catholic Church has been other than intolerant, or that it has ever abstained from persecuting when it was subjected to the old temptation to which it succumbed when it slaughtered the Albigenses and sang Te Deum over the massacre of St. Bartholomew, I do not see the point of these quotations. All Churches have persecuted whenever they have been cursed with the possession of power, and the Church that has had most power has naturally done most persecuting. Logically, the Pope ought perhaps to have burned me if he had got a fair chance, and no doubt there can be ample store of texts exhumed from Papal deliverances that would justify almost any enormity in the shape of persecution. That does

o

not matter to me so much. The caterpillar has been a caterpillar, no doubt, with a voracious appetite for cabbage leaves; but that does not prevent its developing into a radiant butterfly, that sips nectar and lives in the sunshine. The Roman Church, like all other institutions composed of mortal men, is subject to the inevitable law of progress and evolution. It may boast as it pleases of being eternally the same. No system can stereotype a creed which exists in the hearts of living men. The form may be jealously preserved, the spirit is transformed. Men may say they believe in the same things, but their whole perspective insensibly changes, and the real active belief of humanity varies inside and outside the Church from century to century. As all forms of religious belief but represent the angles at which man looks at God, so every change in the mental, moral, and material position of the race modifies its conception of the Infinite. From this law the Roman Church can no more exempt itself than it can refuse to whirl round the sun with the other inhabitants of our planet. It will, of course, by the law of its being, make heroic efforts to preserve a sense of continuity in the mutations through which it passes, and it will naturally repudiate indignantly all accusations of having changed. Even when it is accepting the new doctrine, it will protest most vehe- mently its devotion to the outgrown truth. Of this we have illustrations enough and to spare in the Encyclicals of the present Pope. No one has asserted in more un- compromising terms than he the duty of the State con-

stituted on a Christian basis to establish the Catholic
religion, to favour it, to protect it, and cover it with the
authority of the laws, and not to institute or decree anything which is incompatible with its security. So far
from condescending to acknowledge liberty of thought,
the Pope tells us plainly that "that faculty of thinking
whatever you like, and expressing whatever you like to
think in writing, without any thought of moderation, is
not of its own nature a good in which human society
can rightly rejoice, but, on the contrary, a fount and
origin of many ills." And so far from pretending that
the Papacy is tolerant of liberty of worship, Leo XIII.,
after quoting various Encyclicals, says : " From these
decisions of the Popes it is clearly to be understood that
. . . . it is a crime for private individuals and a
crime for States . . . to treat different kinds of
religion in the same way, that the uncontrolled power
of thinking and publicly proclaiming one's thoughts has
no place amongst the rights of citizens." Again: "The
Church judges it not lawful that the various kinds of
divine worship should have the same right as the true
religion,"—the Catholic to wit. All this, of course, is
intolerance pure and undisguised. That is the old un-
adulterated doctrine of sacerdotal ascendency, which
would have its logical outcome in the *auto da fé*. It is
one of the drawbacks of the continuity of the Church,
that its Popes are constantly embarrassed in their
attempts to reconcile themselves to the age in which
they live by all these monstrous survivals from the age

when men roasted each other for the love of God, and plied the rack and the thumbscrew for the sake of pure religion. But the Church sloughs its faggots and its thumbscrews, even when professing to swear by them. In the very Encyclical from which I have quoted these lamentable specimens of Roman intolerance, the wily and dexterous Pope succeeds with more than Gladstonian agility in extricating himself from his dilemma. It is true that the Popes have caused it clearly to be understood that the State is bound to wield the sword of Cæsar against the enemies of the Church; but, he points out, this is only when the philosophy of the Gospel governed the constitution of the State, and it is only under the Christian order of civil society, now most fortunately for us heretics practically non-existent, that these Papal maxims of intolerance have to be applied. For all serious purposes, we might as well discuss what would take place in space of four dimensions.

More important, because universally applicable, is the doctrine which the Pope lays down as governing the duty of the Church in relation to States not governed by the philosophy of the Gospel—that is to say, to every modern State. Here is the formula by which the Church is enabled to give its formal sanction to religious liberty, and to trample under foot its own old-time doctrine of religious persecution :—

" If, indeed, the various kinds of divine worship are treated as of equal right with the true religion, the Church declares this to be unlawful; but it does not for that reason condemn those rulers of public affairs who, for the sake of attaining some great good, or of averting some evil, patiently endure in custom and practice that each of these kinds of religion should have its place in the commonwealth. For this the Church with all care forbids that any man should be forced against his will to embrace the Catholic faith, as St. Augustine wisely warns us 'that no man can believe unless he be willing.' "

That is, as the *Tablet* was careful at the time to point out—

" An enunciation of great breadth, forasmuch as there is not at this time any people which retains its perfect religious unity. Leo XIII., looking upon the face of Christian Europe, lays down the great laws which govern the Church in the midst of our manifold divisions. It tolerates what it cannot cure, and it disclaims all desire or will to seek for unity by coercion."

" The grapes are sour," sneers the Protestant. It may be so; but, under whatever pretext, is it not good that the fox abandons his attempt to rob the vineyard?

Of course it is easy to complain of this mere absence of condemnation of rulers, who patiently endure in custom and in practice the free exercise of religious worship, as a meagre acknowledgment of the great principle of religious liberty; but it is unscientific to expect your caterpillar to become a butterfly all at a bound. Neither is it good policy to thrust a demonstration down a man's throat, every time he shows an inclination to adopt a more rational view, that his new belief is grossly inconsistent with his former superstitions. Rather is it the part of a judicious friend to encourage the new departure, saying nothing about the inconsistency of the

new truth with the old fallacy, but confidently relying
upon the efficacy of the former to cast out the latter.
Logically, the interdict upon forcing men against their
will to embrace Catholicism carries with it the negative
of the principle of persecution.   When doctors disagree,
the people decide; and when the same Encyclical lays
down principles which logically lead to opposite con-
clusions, it is surely better to lay stress upon those with
which we are in accord than upon those with which we
are in antagonism.

People persist in imagining the Church of Rome to
be either an entirely divine institution or one entirely
diabolic. In reality, it is intensely human, full of incon-
sistencies, paradoxes, and seeming contradictions.   In
the jungle of *obiter dicta* of successive Popes, the ingenious Catholic who is in sympathy with the spirit of
the age finds it easy to find many passages which con-
cede all that he needs in order to reconcile his religion
and his reason. It is true that there are many hard
sayings impossible to harmonise with the more enlightened declarations.   Here, for instance, is one which is
uncompromising enough :—

"As regards opinion, it is necessary both to hold all things
whatsoever the Roman Pontiffs have delivered or shall hereafter
deliver with firm grasp and clear apprehension, and also, as often
as occasion demands, openly to profess the same.   And to give an
instance concerning those things which are called recently-acquired
liberties, it is proper to stand by the judgment of the Apostolic
See, and for every one to hold what she holds."

That, of course, must go far to reducing to blank

despair many a devout Catholic, who can no more accept many of the declarations of the Popes than they can believe that two and two make five. But in the same Encyclical there is this comforting assurance: "Since every true thing must necessarily proceed from God, whatever of truth is by search attained, the Church acknowledges as a certain token of the Divine Mind."

Clearly there is comfort here, and this passage may serve as a sheet anchor to many a troubled spirit.

Of course, it will be said that these are forced interpretations, that it is unfair to lay stress upon the passages which here and there conflict with the whole tendency of the teachings of the Pope. But when there is darkness in all the land. men are justified in fixing their gaze upon the faint rays of light in the east which herald the coming day.

The teaching of the Holy See in respect to democracy must often seem hopelessly irrational to the American prelates, who, to do them justice, seldom lose an opportunity of declaring their belief in a sense exactly contrary to that of the Pope. For while Archbishop Ireland exulted in his great sermon before the Centennial Conference of Catholics at Baltimore, that we lived in a democratic age, in which even princes wished to do the will of the people, the Pope has condemned this assertion as little short of atheistic.

"The idea prevails," he wrote in pious horror in his Encyclical, "that princes are really nothing but delegates to carry out the popular will! In this way it is clear a State

is nothing else but a mob, which is mistress and direc-
tress of itself." As for the fundamental English principle, that resistance to tyrants is obedience towards
God, the Pope regards it as utterly damnable. "To
cast away obedience, and by popular violence to incite
to sedition, is treason not only against man but against
God." That so-called "sedition" may be the first duty
of a Christian and a patriot has not yet dawned upon
the Holy See. The great republic that was cradled in
rebellion, and the race that established its liberties by
revolution, can never listen with patience to the pious
platitudes of Encyclicals concerning the heinousness of
resistance to tyranny. But even here there are signs of
dawning reason. It is true that the Pope, wringing his
hands, declares, "Verily things under the auspices of
these doctrines [of modern democracy] have come to
such a pass, that many sanction this as a law in civil
jurisprudence, to wit, that sedition may rightly be raised;"
but in a still later Encyclical, that of 1888, the Pope
lays down doctrines concerning the right of resistance
to oppression which would delight the heart of a Puritan
or a Republican :

"If, then, by any power, there be sanctioned anything out of
conformity with the principles of right reason, which is consequently hurtful to the commonwealth, such an enactment can have
no authority as not being even a law of justice, but likely to lead
men away from that good which is the only end of civil society.
Where the power to command is wanting, or where a law is
enacted contrary to reason, or to the eternal law, or the ordinance
of God, obedience is unlawful, lest while obeying man we fail in
obedience to God." Again—"Wherever there exists or there is

reason to fear either an unjust oppression of the people or a depriva-
tion of the Church's liberty, it is lawful to seek for such a change
of Government as will give due liberty of action."

That is good and sound, and, carried to its logical conclusion, will justify every "sedition" that was ever justly
raised by an oppressed people against an oppressive
Government. Then, again, while American Catholics
must writhe when they read such blasphemy against the
American Constitution as the Pope's *obiter dicta*, that
the doctrine of the supremacy of the people is in contradiction to reason, and that the absurdity of the position
of those who hold the fatal theory of the separation of
Church and State is manifest, they can gather comfort from
the declaration in the same Encyclical, that "it is not of
itself wrong to prefer a democratic form of Government,
if only the Catholic doctrine be maintained as to the
origin and use of power. Neither does the Church condemn those who, if it can be done without violation of
justice, wish to make their country independent of any
foreign or despotic power."

So it is all through. "The oracle speaks with a
double voice; you pay your money and take your
choice." The Papal Encyclical upon Liberty is sufficiently uncompromising in form. Liberty of worship,
it declares, is opposed to the virtue of religion, and is the
abject subjection of the soul to sin. Liberty of the
press is not right, for false doctrines should be diligently
repressed by public authority. Under unbridled license
of speech and of writing, nothing will remain sacred,

and so forth. As for liberty of teaching, it is opposed to reason, and tends to pervert men's minds. All teaching, even of science, where it appears to bear on faith and morals, must be subject to the just and necessary restraint of the judgment of the Church. Liberty of conscience is only permissible when it is used in a Christian sense. Yet in this very Encyclical there occurs a passage which opens the door wide to all these liberties. Here it is:

"With the discernment of a true mother, the Church weighs the great burden of human weakness, and she knows what is the course in which the minds and the affairs of men are now borne along. For this reason, while not conceding any rights to anything that is not true and honest, it does not forbid public authority to tolerate what is at variance with truth and justice, for the sake of avoiding a greater evil, or of obtaining or preserving some greater good."

This doctrine of the pitying mother who understands the tendency of the times, and tolerates in practice what she condemns in theory, enables the Pope to execute a curve with rapidity and dignity. Not, of course, that he admits the curve:

"Although, in the extraordinary condition of these times, the Church usually acquiesces in certain modern liberties, not because she prefers them in themselves, but because she judges it expedient to permit them, in better times she would use her liberty."

And be as intolerant as ever, no doubt. But, fortunately for the Church, such "better times" will return no more for ever.

The real hope of the Church lies in the new world of English speakers, who are bringing into the fold the beliefs and aspirations of our democratic, self-governing, self-reliant race. Of the Latin nations, it may be said in relation to the English, as was spoken by John the Baptist about the Messiah, "They must decrease—we must increase." The Pope may not like democracy and the Anglo-American ideas. St. Peter as a fisherman, accustomed to the fresh-water boating of the Lake of Gennesaret, would probably have shrunk from sailing in the salt sea, much as the Pope shrinks from democracy. But he would never have got to Rome if he had not crossed the brine. Neither will his successor ever attain the headship of the modern world unless he reconciles himself with the democratic spirit now supreme through all English-speaking lands. That which is important in the Encyclicals is that which opens the door to modern ideas. The anathemas do not count. These are mere dead leaves and outward husks, whose decay manures the plant that will spring from the seed, in which alone there is life. Who, it may be asked, can say which is the vital germ in all these voluminous Encyclicals? The vital germ is that which can survive best in the conditions of its new environment. Hence, if we look at the environment which will govern the survival or the elimination of the various principles now existing more or less side by side in the Papal teachings, we may discover without much difficulty what is husk and what is germ. Already the influence of the spirit of the English speaker has made itself felt in the Church in England, in the States, and in the Colonies. There is so little of the mediæval tophamper retained in English Catholic Churches, that an English Catholic must often be almost as much shocked as an English Puritan in visiting many of the Churches of Rome. In England and in America we have already a humanised Catholicism, which is rationalism itself compared with the Bambino worship of Italy. But the best way of illustrating the difference is by reprinting bodily the very remarkable discourse which the Archbishop of St. Paul's, in the North-West, delivered to the Centennial Conference of the American Catholics held this November at Baltimore. Archbishop Ireland is a prelate of high standing and of great influence. As he was selected specially to preach to the Conference on the new century, it is evident that he is generally regarded by his brethren as one who, more than any other, is best fitted to interpret the spirit in which American Catholics face the future. His sermon is so different in spirit, in form, and in substance to the Encyclicals, that it is difficult to believe that the author is actually a faithful and obedient servant of the Church which has the author of the Encyclicals as its chief. Yet this is the fact; and, thanks to the immense increase of English speakers in the world, it is the faith of the Archbishop which will practically dictate the future development of the doctrines of the Pope.

Archbishop Ireland's discourse was on "The new century—responsibilities, hopes, and duties." The text was, "For thy soul fight for justice, and even unto death fight for justice, and God will overthrow thy enemies for thee" (Ecclesiasticus iv. 33). His Grace

said : A century closes ; a century opens. The present is for
Catholics in America a most solemn moment. Another speaker
has reviewed the past, evoked from its shades the spirits of its
heroes, and read to you the lessons of their labours. I will bid you
turn to the future. It has special significance for us. The past our
fathers wrought; the future will be wrought by us. The next century of the Church in America will be what we make it. It will be
our own—the fruit of our labours. Oh, for a prophet's eye to
glance adown the unborn years, and from now to read the story of
God's Church on this continent as generations a hundred years
hence may read it ! But the prophet's eye is not needed. As we
will it, so shall the story be. Brothers—bishops, priests, laymen,
in what words can I tell the responsibility which weighs upon us?
—there is so much at stake for God and souls, for Church and
country ; there is so much in dependency upon our co-operation
with the Divine action in the world. The duty of the moment,
surely, is to understand this responsibility, and to do the full work
which Heaven has allotted to us—for our souls to strive for justice,
and even unto death to fight for justice. It is our own work. I
would sink deeply into our souls the vital truth that the
work which is to be done is our work. With us it will be
done; without us it will not be done. And there is sore need that
Catholics ponder well this truth. Not in theory but in practice,
the error obtains among them, that in matters religious man has
scarcely aught to do, the work being done by God. Do not
imagine that I lose sight of the absolute necessity of the Divine
act. The teaching of faith is not forgotten, that "unless the Lord
build the house, they labour in vain who build it." But no less is
it the teaching of faith that in producing results the human must
blend with the Divine, and the absence of the one renders the other
sterile. Too often we do not do our part ; we seem to wish that
God do all. God will not alter the rulings of His providence to
make up for our inaction.

There are times in the history of the Church when the need is
that insistance be made on the supernatural in the work of the
Church. There are times when the need is that insistance be made
on the natural. Singular phenomenon of our times! In all matters
outside religion, the natural has unlimited play, and draws out for

action its most hidden energies ; in religion it looks as if the natural
sought to extinguish itself, so as to leave the entire field to the
supernatural.   There are countries where the faithful Catholics
pray, administer and receive the Sacraments, and are afraid to go a
few steps farther.   I cannot name the country where they are fully
alive to their opportunities and their duties.   Do American Catholics put into the work of religion the sleepless energy and the
boundless heartiness that characterise them in secular affairs?   As
we often are and often do, failure in religion is inevitable.   God
will save His Church in all times. This He has promised.   But no
promise was given as to the splendour of her reign, or as to her
permanent dwelling among a particular people.   The apocalyptic
candlestick has often been moved from its place.   There are bright
and there are dark lines in the Church's history.   God always did
His part ; man's part was not always done.   When saints walked
upon the earth, their pathway sparkled with rays of light from
heaven, and the surrounding atmosphere was made ablaze.   What
shall be the lines in our own century of the Church's history?   God
demands that we make answer.

Let me state, as I conceive it, the great work which, in God's
providence, the Catholics of the United States are called to do
within the coming century.   It is twofold :—To make America
Catholic, and to solve for the Church Universal the all-absorbing
problem with which the age confronts her.   I doubt if ever, since
that century the dawn of which was the glimmer from Eastern star,
there was prepared for Catholics of any nation of earth a work so
grandly noble in its nature and pregnant with such mighty consequences.   The conversion of America should be ever present to the
minds of Catholics in America, as a supreme duty from which God
will not hold them exempt.   It is a providential nation.   How
youthful, and yet how great ! How rich in glorious promise ! The
most daring elements of other lands have come hither to form a
new people—new in energy, new in spirit, new in action—in complete adaptation to the new epoch in the world's history through
which we are living.   We cannot but believe that a singular
mission is assigned to America, glorious for ourselves, and beneficent to the whole race, that of bringing forth a new social and
political order, based, more than any other that has heretofore

existed, upon the common brotherhood of man, and more than any other securing to the multitude of the people social happiness and equality of rights. In our own are bound up the hopes of the billions of the whole earth. The Church triumphant in America, Catholic truth will travel on the wings of American influence, and with it encircle the universe. The present time is one of history's great epochs, when the face of the earth is changed. The world is in throes: we are assisting at the birth of a new age. The traditions of the past vanish; new social forms arise, and new political institutions; there are astounding discoveries of the secrets and the powers of nature; unwonted forces are at work in every sphere over which man's control may reach; there is a revolution in the ideas and feelings of men. All things which may be changed will be changed, and nothing will be to-morrow as it was yesterday, save that which emanates directly from God, or which the Eternal decrees to be permanent.

. The movements of the modern world have put before us a startling question. It is none other than this: Will not the Church, an institution of past ages, go down with other legacies of those ages? Why should she alone ride triumphantly above the billows that are sweeping all else into destruction? Is there need of the Church? Is she not, rather, a barrier to the best ambitions and the progressive march of humanity? A reply is urgent. It can be given, for the Church is Divine, and belongs to all ages. But the more speedily and the more effectively we give it, the better for Church and souls.

A study of the modern world brings us to say that its leading feature is a resolute assertion of the powers and rights of nature, as distinguished from the revealed or supernatural order. The Christian religion displaced in the life of mankind nineteen hundred years ago the reign of corrupt nature known as Paganism. For long ages the supernatural was supreme, permeating minds and hearts, reaching out its influence on social institutions and governments, upon arts and industries, the natural order acting in fullest harmony with its laws and spirit. At the opening of the sixteenth century signs of new times appeared on the horizon. The Renaissance, unconsciously perhaps, sowed in nature the seeds of rebellion. The inevitable reaction from the teachings of the reformers as to the total depravity of fallen nature quickened its spirit of self-assertion.   Then came the wondrous feats and discoveries of the past hundred years, and nature was emboldened, and it proclaimed its self-sufficiency and its independence.

The watchwords of the age are reason, education, liberty, the material improvement of the masses.   Nor are these watchwords empty sounds.   They represent solid realities, for which the age deserves praise.   Rebellious nature lays claim to words and to realities, as if they were its exclusive belonging, obtained not only by its unaided self, but in spite of the supernatural.   War is declared against the Church and all revealed religion, in the name of progress, and of all forward movements ; and combatants, ranged under banners upon which descriptive words are inscribed, easily gather to themselves popular applause.   The war is between the natural and the supernatural.   The intent is to exclude Christ and His Church from the living world ; to relegate them amid ruins and sepulchres, as they once relegated Paganism.   I need not tell the duty of Christians.   It is to maintain in the world the supremacy of the supernatural, and save the age to the Church.   The burthen of the strife falls to the lot of Catholics in America.   The movements of the modern world have their highest tension in the United States.   The natural order is here seen at its best, and here displays its fullest strength.   Here, too, the Church, unhampered by dictate of Government, or by despotic custom, can, with the freedom of the Son of Isai [Jesse], choose its arms, and making straight for the opposing foe, bring the contest to speedier close.   The Church to-day, as when she overthrew Pagan Rome, and won over to grace ferocious Northmen, is the Church of Divine truth and Divine power.   Her mission is to-day, as then, to teach all nations, to preach the Gospel to every creature, and Christ is with her, even unto the consummation of ages.   God's arm is not shortened.   What can be wanting ?   Our own resolute will to put to profit God's graces and God's opportunities.   " For thy soul fight for justice ; even unto death strive for justice, and God will overthrow thy enemies."

Of inestimable advantage to us is the liberty the Church enjoys under the constitution of the Republic.   No tyrant here casts chains around her ; no concordat limits her action, or cramps her energies. She is as free as the eagle upon Alpine heights, free to spread out in unobstructed flight her pinions, to soar to highest altitudes, to put into action all her native energies. The law of the land protects her in her rights, and asks in return no sacrifice of these rights, for her rights are those of American citizenship. The Republic at its very birth guaranteed liberty to Catholics, at a time when, in nearly all other lands, Protestant and Catholic governments were oppressing her, and during her whole history she has not failed to make good her guarantee. This present day, in how few lands, outside our own, the Church is really free. If great things are not done by Catholics in America, the fault lies surely with themselves—not with the Republic.

The tendencies and movements of the age, which affright the timid, are providential opportunities, opening the way for us to most glorious victory. That modern ideas and movements are under all their aspects deserving of approval, I am far from asserting. They are often, in one way or another, immoral and iniquitous, and Pius IX. has warned us that as they come before as the Church cannot be reconciled to them. And yet how much there is in them that is grand and good! Despite its defects and its mistakes, I love my age. I love its aspirations and its resolves. I revel in its feats of valour, its industries, and its discoveries. I thank it for its many benefactions to my fellowmen, to the people rather than to princes and rulers. I seek no backward voyage across the sea of time. I will ever press forward. I believe that God intends the present to be better than the past, and the future to be better than the present. We should live in our age, know it, be in touch with it. There are Catholics more numerous, however, in Europe than in America, to whom the present will not be known until long after it shall become the past. Our work is in the present and not in the past. It will not do to understand the thirteenth better than the nineteenth century; to be more conversant with the errors of Arius or Eutyches than with those of contemporary infidels or agnostics; to study more deeply the causes of Albigensian or Lutheran heresies, or the French Revolution, than the causes of the social upheavals of our own times. The world has entered into an entirely new phase; the past will not return; reaction is the dream of men who see not and hear not;

P

who sit at the gates of cemeteries weeping over tombs that shall not be re-opened, in utter oblivion of the living world back of them. We should speak to our age—of things it feels and the language it understands. We should be in it and of it, if we should have its ear. For the same reasons there is needed a thorough sympathy with the country. I would have Catholics be the first patriots in the land.

It is an intellectual age. It worships intellect. All things are tried by the touchstone of intellect, and the ruling power, public opinion, is formed by it. The Church will be judged by the standard of intellect. Catholics must excel in religious knowledge. They must be in the foreground of all intellectual movements. An important work for Catholics in the coming century will be the building up of schools, colleges, and seminaries ; and, what is still more important, the lifting up of present and future institutions to the highest degree of intellectual excellence. Only the best schools will give the Church the men she needs. Modern, too, they must be in curriculum and method, so that pupils emerging from their halls will be men for the twentieth century and men for America. In love, in reverence, in hope I salute the Catholic University of America, whose birth—happy omen !—is coeval with the opening of our new century. The destinies of the Church in America are in thy keeping, school of our hopes ! May heaven's light shine over thee, and heaven's love guard thee ! I do not forget the vast importance for the Church of Catholic literature and of the Catholic press. They, too, are schools, and schools not only for the days of youth, but for the entire time of life, and they deserve, and should obtain, our warmest encouragement.

The strength of the Church to-day in all countries, particularly in America, is the people. This is essentially the age of democracy. The days of princes and of feudal lords are gone ; monarchs hold their thrones to execute the will of the people. Woe to religion where this fact is not understood ! He who holds the masses reigns. The masses are held by their intellect and their heart. No power controls them, save that which touches their own free souls. We have a dreadful lesson to learn from certain European countries, in which, from weight of tradition, the Church clings to thrones and classes, and loses her grasp upon the people. Let us

not make this mistake. It is time to bring back the primitive
Gospel spirit, to go out into highways and byways, to preach on
house-tops and in market-places. Erect stately churches if you
will; they are grand monuments to religion, but be they filled
with people. If all are not there, press the absentees to hear you
beneath humbler roofs. If some remain yet outside, speak to them
in the streets or the public road. The time has come for "salvation armies" to penetrate the wildest thicket of thorns and briers,
and bring God's word to the ear of the most vile, the most ignorant, and the most godless. Saving those who insist on being
saved, as we are satisfied in doing, is not the mission of the
Church. "Compel them to come in" is the command of the
Master. This is not the religion we need to-day—to sing lovely
anthems in cathedral stalls and wear copes of broidered gold,
while no multitude throng the nave or aisle, and the world outside
is dying of spiritual and moral starvation. Seek out men; speak
to them, not in stilted phrase or seventeenth century sermon style,
but in burning words that go to their hearts as well as their minds.
Popularise religion, so far as principle admits; make the people
chant in holy exultation canticles of praise and adoration; draw
them to God by all the chords of Adam. Save the masses. Cease
not planning and working for their salvation.

The care of the masses implies an abiding and active interest in
the social questions that torment at the present time humanity.
Our chieftain, Leo XIII., who knows his age, and whose heart-
beatings are in sympathy with it, has told Catholics their duties on
this point. Leo XIII. speaks fearlessly to the world of the rights
of labour; Cardinal Lavigerie pleads for the African slave; Cardinal Manning interposes his hand between the plutocratic merchant
and the working-man of the docks; Count de Mun and his band of
noble-minded friends devote talent and time to the interest of
French labourers. As a body, we are quietness itself. We say our
prayers, we preach, we listen to sermons on the love of God, and
resignation in suffering; or, if we venture into the arena, it is at the
eleventh hour, when others have long before preceded us, and public
opinion is already formed. Singular is all this! Christ made the
social question the very basis of His ministry. "The blind see, the
lame walk, the lepers are cleansed, and the poor have the Gospel

preached to them." The Church in her whole past history grappled with every social problem that came in her way and solved it. What has come over us that we shun the work which is essentially ours? These are days of warfare, days of action. It is not the age of the timid and fugitive virtue of the Thebaid. Into the arena, priest and layman! Seek out social grievances; lead in movements to heal them. Peep mercifully into factories, at etiolated youth and infancy. Breathe fresh air into the crowded tenement quarters of the poor. Follow upon the streets the crowds of vagrant children. Lessen on railways and in public service Sunday work, which renders for thousands the practice of religion impossible. Cry out against the fearful evil of intemperance, which is damning hourly the bodies and souls of countless victims. "This is religion pure and undefiled." This will secure the age to God's Church.

What I have heretofore said applies to all—to priests, who as leaders must be first in act as well as in command, and also, in greater part at least, to laymen. But lest I be misunderstood in a matter of such importance, I now make to laymen a special and emphatic appeal. Priests are officers; you are soldiers. There is on the part of Catholic laymen too much leaning upon priests. If priests work, laymen imagine they can rest. In Protestantism, where there is no firm, constituted ministerial organisation, the layman feels more his responsibility, and there is often witnessed strong lay action. In America in the present age lay action is particularly needed for the Church. Laymen have in this age a special vocation. My words have borne on the exterior life of Catholics. This point I desire to emphasise. I am speaking to men of action, to soldiers, whom I would arouse to deeds of highest valour. God forbid that I forget the needs of interior Christian life. Without this, we are at best but sounding brass and tinkling cymbals, and however much we may plant and water, God will not give the growth. Nor do I forget that, however much I desire you to do for others, your first and all-important duty is to yourselves, to save your own souls. And now, brethren, the new century opens. We remit it into the hands of Almighty God. Oh, God, bless and guard in special love Thy holy Church. Bless and guard the Republic of the United States.

So far the eloquent prelate. If we read the Encyclicals in the light of those words, if we clearly grasp the fact that it is men who speak as Archbishop Ireland speaks, and who feel as he feels, who will dominate the world, we shall not have much difficulty in arriving at a sound conclusion as to what in the Encyclicals is but as stubble for the burning, and what is destined to survive and flourish—that is, of course, if the Church itself is not to dwindle into a mere historical curiosity, possessing only the antiquarian interest of a superior kind of Egyptian mummy.

CHAPTER XIV.

THE NEXT POPE—INTERVIEW WITH CARDINAL PAROCCHI.

THE accession of Pius the Ninth was predicted by a famous prophetess, known as Rosa Columba of Taggia, a little village in the Riviera, just before you reach Ventimiglia, on the frontier between France and Italy. But no prophetess or prophet has named the successor of Leo. The good woman of Taggia, however, has left a prophecy behind her which still remains to be fulfilled. She died in 1837. When Cardinal Manning first visited Italy in 1848 he was told of her prophecies, which events almost immediately began to fulfil. Among other predictions, this simple villager is said to have foretold that Louis Philippe would lose his throne and die in exile; that Charles Albert would be driven from his kingdom and die in exile; that the Pope Pius would be driven from Rome, but would be restored by Napoleon. "Silly woman!" cried those to whom she repeated the vision. "Napoleon is dead." Events, however, vindicated her prediction to the letter. Rosa Columba further prophesied that there would be a war between Austria and Sardinia, in which the latter would be defeated, and

then that there would be another war in which Austria
would be defeated. Then would come a revolution in
Italy, after which a kingdom of Italy would be set up.
Every one of these predictions has been fulfilled. They
were taken down from the woman's lips in the presence
of the Bishop of Ventimiglia, who was questioned on the
subject by Cardinal Manning during the Vatican Council,
and who fully confirmed the story in every particular.
But the full tale of Rosa Columba's prophecies is not yet
told. She went on to say that there would be another
Revolution in Italy. Then there is to be a great European war, and—curious detail this—in the course of the
campaign the Russian soldiers would stable their horses
in the church of the convent at Taggia.

The speculations of the cognoscenti as to the probable
choice of the College of Cardinals belong to a different
but hardly more trustworthy class of prophecies than the
visions of Rosa Columba. But unless the well-informed
are more than usually at fault, there can be little doubt
that at this moment the chances are heavy that the next
Conclave will install Cardinal Parocchi in the Papal
chair. There has been some talk about electing an
English-speaking Cardinal to the post. It is so much
idle wind. Cardinal Gibbons would no doubt be a
vigorous American Pope, but at present the rule is absolute at the Vatican—"No non-Italians need apply." The
primacy of the Church is one of the perquisites of the
Italian peninsula. Cardinal Parocchi is thought to have
the field to himself. He is secure to have from 28 to 34

votes in the present College, so I was told; and if so, his election is a foregone conclusion. There are only sixty Cardinals at present, and not more than fifty could attend the Conclave. If Cardinal Parocchi can command forty votes, he will be elected. But, for my own part, I reserve judgment. Nothing is more uncertain than the voting in the Conclave, and I will believe that Cardinal Parocchi will be the next Pope when I hear of his election.

But although the result may falsify calculations, the fact that common report points him out with such unanimity as the probable successor of Leo XIII. shows that Cardinal Parocchi is one of the most conspicuous personalities in the Roman Curia. Cardinal Parocchi is Vicar-General of Rome, and as such he holds his Court for the Pope in spiritual matters concerning the diocese of Rome at No. 70 Via della Scrofa. He is a Cardinal with a history. When he was appointed Bishop of Bologna, he was refused his *exequatur* by the Italian Government; so that, although he was duly appointed Bishop by the Pope, he could not draw the emoluments of the See. The refusal of the Italian Government to allow him to be legally instituted at Bologna was really due to a faction in the city, which intrigued against Cardinal Parocchi, and created sufficient ill-blood against him to lead to this somewhat exceptional step on the part of the Government of the Quirinal. No *exequatur*, however, being required for the assumption of the duties of Vicar-General in Rome, Cardinal Parocchi was, after a time, transferred to his present responsible post, bringing with him a reputation, perhaps unjustly acquired, of being a cordial enemy to the Italian kingdom. So thoroughly established is that reputation, that he is popularly regarded as a black of the blacks, the most *intransigente* of all the clericals, and the most reactionary in all questions which are at present in dispute between the Quirinal and the Vatican. A rector of one of the English-speaking colleges assured me that this was a mistake—that Cardinal Parocchi had a shrewd head upon his shoulders, full of practical common sense; that he was a very Opportunist for arranging things in order to attain a practical end, and that no mistake could be greater than to regard him as the fanatic of reaction.

After passing through various ante-chambers, almost as if you were entering into the presence of a Sovereign Prince, we were ushered into a large reception-room, where, at the end of a long table, with a crucifix and a picture of the Madonna and Child immediately before him, sat the Vicar-General of Rome. The light was curiously arranged, so that it fell full on the face of his visitors, while his own features remained in the shade. But he was evidently a man of considerable determination, and in the full vigour of life, with a mind active and alert, looking out from beady black eyes under bushy brows. He has a jaw also of immense power. His address was pleasing. He said that he occasionally read the *Pall Mall Gazette*, and inquired, as most people do, how its name was pronounced—whether as Pawl

Mawl or Pell Mell.   After explaining that the *a* is pronounced as though it were *e*, I said I was very glad to
have the opportunity of meeting him, inasmuch as his
position as Vicar-General caused him to be conspicuous
above all the rest of the Roman Cardinals.   This he
modestly disclaimed, declaring it to be much exaggerated,
and adding that we deceived ourselves greatly in England if we accorded him any such pre-eminence.   I
went on to say that the fact that he did occupy such a
position filled us with the more grief, because we understood that it was also reported that he was, of all the
Cardinals, the most opposed to English ideas.   He did
not readily catch my meaning, and thought that I meant
he was non-friendly to England.

Speaking with great animation and considerable
oratorical force and point, he exclaimed, "Hostile to
England!   There is no country that is so near my
heart.   Is it not because of my devotion to England
that I venerate so much the memory of Gregory the
Great, for it was to him that we owe the conversion of
that country?   But," said he, "although I love England,
I do not love oppression, I do not love injustice; and I
must say that in your dealings with Ireland you have
been guilty of both."

"You preach to the converted," I replied; "so far
as Ireland is concerned, you can say nothing too hard
about England's action in that country.   But I was not
speaking of England's power but of English ideas."

"English ideas," said he; "English ideas? What are

English ideas? Surely they are those which fill me with admiration;—the positive spirit of your countrymen, their practical capacity, their energy, all that is distinctively English, I specially esteem. I read Shakespeare and John Milton and John Dryden, those great and glorious classics of your tongue, and I am filled with admiration at the character, the national character, which is reflected in such works, and which they have helped to mould."

"Ah, I see," said I, "you do not understand. By 'English ideas' I mean distinctly the modern idea. The idea of liberty, of progress, and of popular government."

"Ah!" said he, "I am against destruction, that is true."

"But you would approve of destroying that which was evil?"

"True; but I would hold fast to that which is good. But in England you do more than that. I think that the English are in many respects a very conservative nation, much more conservative than I am myself. There are many things in England which you preserve which, if I were in your place, I would entirely change."

"What, for instance?"

"Take one case—the condition of your law. I would codify your law, so that every man would know what the law of his country was. England refuses to do so, and preserves a jungle of precedents and a labyrinth of cases which render it impossible for the ordinary man to know the law of the land which he is bound to obey.   That is one thing in which England is much more conservative than I."

"You have selected a strong instance," I said.   " I am delighted to hear you speak in such a way.   It encourages me to hope that you will not regard with distaste the development which seems to me probable in the future—namely, the transference of the Holy See from Rome to London."

"Ah!" said he, "that is a great question.   It is a great question; but it is a question for the future."

"Yes," I replied; "but it may become practical at any moment.   Your religious orders have been driven from almost every Latin country.   They take refuge with the English-speaking nations.   As the religious orders have had to seek a refuge with us, so it seems to me will the Pope."

"It may be so," said he; "it may be so.   As an Italian, I should be heartbroken at the thought of the Holy See leaving my native country; but if in the providence of God the Holy Father should be driven forth to a foreign land, there is no country to whose hospitality and to whose respect for religion I would go more gladly than to England.   Yes," said he, meditatively, "yes, you have shown the world an example.   I am constantly repeating ' Liberty as in London and as in New York,' ' Liberty as in London and as in New York '—that is my watchword."

Naturally, I expressed my gratification at hearing so

emphatic a sentiment from the lips of him whom I had been instructed to expect as the blackest of blacks, and the most utterly hopeless of all the clerical reactionaries. "To turn to another subject," said I, "I believe you are the only Cardinal who has ever been a journalist?"

"A journalist?" he replied. "No, that I cannot say."

"But did you edit some journal at Bologna?"

"No," said he, "not a journal, but a magazine, which appeared periodically, which was devoted to literature, philosophy, and such subjects, and not to news."

"I regret this, for I thought that, as a journalist, you would sympathize with what I have been saying at the Vatican concerning its neglect of the press."

"I am delighted to hear it," said he. "I am delighted to hear that you have been speaking at the Vatican on that subject. I hope you will cry aloud and lift up your voice; you cannot speak too loudly about it. I have screamed myself hoarse on the subject. It is most important."

"My idea was," I explained, "that a good deal might be done short of the establishment of an organ of the Vatican——"

"But that also has been contemplated," he interrupted. "A short time ago we had arrangements almost completed for the publication of a great international journal at Rome, which was to have been tetraglot— that is, to have been published in four languages, Italian, French, English, German — a journal whose function would have been to have disseminated the truth, and to have defended the Holy See against its enemies, and still more against its friends, who are much the more dangerous."

"Then the scheme has been abandoned?"

"Postponed, rather. It was thought well that at present we should preserve an attitude of reserve and quiescence. It would require, of course, a great capital, and for the moment the scheme has been adjourned."

"It seems to me that, pending the establishment of such a great journal, it would be well to establish, both in the interests of the Vatican and of the journalists of the world, a bureau which could communicate every week or oftener, as the case might be, authentic information, which at the present moment lies unused in the pigeon-holes of the Vatican."

"An excellent idea, and I hope that you will do all you can to convince them of the importance of carrying it out."

"Now," said I, coming on to delicate ground, "might I ask what is your view as to the Temporal Power? Report says that you are so devoted to the sovereignty of the Pope that you would even sanction a war for its restoration."

He drew back. "Upon that subject, I hope you will allow me to preserve my opinions in the recesses of my breast. But I may say that it is not a practical question. There is no question of a war for the re-establishment of the Temporal Power. The only war to which I am committed, and on which I would concentrate all the energies of the Church, is the war against vice, against crime, against ignorance. These are the foes against which we would contend. That is the only war of which I approve."

"Now," said I, "there is one last question on which I should like to ask your opinion. That is, concerning the position of woman."

He brightened up instantly and exclaimed, "I often say that there is no room for respect where there is no liberty for action. Nobody can be said to respect woman who does not leave her free to act."

"An admirable saying," said I, "which I am rejoiced to hear from your lips."

"Why should you be surprised?" said he. "Is it not entirely in accordance with the genius, with the fundamental principles of the Catholic Church?" Pointing to the picture of the Madonna in front of him, he continued, "There is Our Lady, whom we place at the summit of all creatures; and throughout, the whole organization is the same. Everywhere the importance of women is recognised from the highest down to the lowest. Look at our great religious orders, which have been founded by women, are managed and controlled by women. Their superiors have in all things the same rights, positions, and authorities as in the religious orders founded by men. After all, what is it that woman wants? She wants a career. She requires opportunities in which to develop and employ all her faculties, all her capacities. As for the question of woman suffrage, that is a mere detail. If, in the modern state, it is necessary for woman to possess the franchise, in order to enable her to develop all her faculties and to achieve a career, then far be it from me to oppose woman suffrage. There are no figures in history which command my admiration more than the great heroines who from time to time have arisen to direct and control the affairs of nations. There was Joan of Arc in France, there was Isabel of Castille, and " — with a roguish twinkle in his eye — " there was your own Elizabeth of England, who, notwithstanding her red hair and her numerous little *faux pas*, was greatly admired by Sixtus the Fifth. Who would not wish that there should be more such women, capable of playing a great rôle in the affairs of the world? Ah, who would not prefer to be governed by a wise and courageous woman than by a weak, foolish man?"

By this time I had heard all that I could possibly hope to obtain from Cardinal Parocchi, and as the antechamber was full of people waiting for an audience, I took my leave.

CHAPTER XV.

WHAT WE MAY HOPE FROM ROME.

I now proceed to summarise as succinctly as I can the substance of what I was told in the Vatican by the representatives of the policy of the Papacy.

I. *The Temporal Power.*—On this subject I was officially authorised to declare, in the most authoritative manner possible, that the Pope is utterly and absolutely opposed to any attack being made upon Italy for the purpose of restoring his Temporal Power by force of arms. I am assured on the highest authority that, so far from the pamphlet, "The Truth about the Roman Question," being an official or officious or authentic exponent of the views of the Pope on this subject, the Holy Father repudiates in the strongest possible terms the indiscreet and criminal declaration that every good Catholic would applaud any power which attacked Italy to restore the Temporal Power. The Pope desires peace. He would regard any appeal to the sword on his behalf as a crime. So long as there is any kind of order kept in Rome, the Holy Father will energetically oppose any and every proposal to use armed force to

Q.

re-establish his kingdom. He would rather remain a prisoner in the Vatican till he died than that one sword should be unsheathed to restore his Temporal Power. Nothing could be more explicit than the terms used to authorise me to declare publicly, in the name of the Pope, that his Holiness regards all those who, in speech or in print, advocate war against Italy for his sake as the enemies of the Holy See, who are acting in diametrical opposition to his solemnly proclaimed will—of which let all bellicose French priests and journalists take due note. They are the enemies of the Pope, and are so regarded by the Holy Father himself, if in word or deed they incite to any attack upon the Italian kingdom for the sake of re-establishing his Temporal Sovereignty. So far as explicit and authoritative declarations go, nothing could possibly be more satisfactory in the interests of the general peace than the assurances I received in the Vatican.

II. *The Future Seat of the Holy See.*—When, some months ago, I declared that if the Catholic Church were to wield the ascendency in the New Era that it exerted in the old, it would have to shift its capital westward to English-speaking lands, it was regarded as a somewhat daring flight of fancy. I do not regard it in that light to-day. Nothing, of course, has been decided upon. The Pope will not quit Rome as long as he can cling to the Vatican. But I was assured most categorically that if he were, by Divine providence, forced to flee for his life from the See of St. Peter, he would confidently count upon receiving a hospitable welcome under the British flag. If he left Rome, the jealousies of the Catholic nations are so great that he would be almost necessarily driven to find shelter in a Protestant State. At present the talk is all of Malta, where Sir J. Lintorn Simmons, it is believed, has suggested that the Pope might find a retreat. But Malta is not conveniently accessible, and after Malta there is no place like London. The religious orders, driven from one Latin nation after another, have taken refuge in England. If the Pope should be driven from Italy, he will find his Avignon on the banks of the Thames.

III.—*Home Rule and Redistribution.*—The Pope has partially learnt the need of Home Rule, and the danger of autocratic centralisation, from the disappointments which his attempts to dictate to the Catholics of Ireland and of Germany have brought upon him in the last few years. It is understood that he will not again take any action in Irish politics without consulting the Irish bishops, both those who are in Ireland and those who are beyond the sea. The more the Pope deals in realities of everyday life, the more he will be compelled to defer to the men on the spot who know these facts. Centralisation of the old style is only possible in things celestial and invisible. In things terrestrial, where the laws of arithmetic and dynamics hold good, he can take no liberties with impunity; and he must therefore develop the precedent set by his Irish resolution, and allow greater latitude, and accord greater responsibility to his

representatives, who are face to face with the practical
realities of the question at issue.   The desire of the
Irish for the appointment of a duly accredited elected
Irish representative at the Vatican, who should never
be more than six months out of Ireland at a time,
without whom no action should be taken in Irish
matters, was regarded as inadmissible.   The need
for increasing the representation of other nations in the
Sacred College was frankly admitted; but so long as the
Holy See is domiciled in Italy, the over-representation
of the Italians will not be seriously impaired.   If an increasing number of non-Italian ecclesiastics enter for the
career of administrators in the Church, the process will
go on at an accelerated rate.   At present the Pope, with
the best will in the world, would find a difficulty in finding men outside Italy, competent for learning and education, to fill the posts which are at present monopolised
by Italians.

IV.— *The Utilisation of the Press.*—Herein I think I
see light.   The Pope has not yet organized a Correspondence Bureau of the Vatican, which would supply the
newspapers of the world with a polyglot correspondence.
But already a beginning has been made, unofficially, it
is true, but still a beginning, and I am not without hopes
that journalism and the Church may before long be in
closer relationship.   The salary paid to a single super-
numerary canon of St. Peter's, who does nothing but
sing his breviary—no one listening—would suffice to lay
on into every newspaper office in Christendom a weekly

sheet of the news and the views of the Vatican.   Nor is
it only in this direction that we may expect Rome to
move.   Her own clergy need the stimulus of the weekly
paper direct from headquarters.   For £4,000 per
annum 10,000 copies of a four-page daily paper can be
printed and delivered by post six days a week in every
part of Italy.   For the purpose of keeping the opinions
of the Holy Father constantly before his faithful priests
and laymen, it is simply incredible that so cheap and
effective a means of education and of propaganda should
have been so scandalously neglected.   If once the Holy
See begins to use the Press in earnest, with its agents in
every village and its bookstall in every Church, the circulation of the *Petit Journal* itself would be nowhere
compared with the millions of copies of the sheet
which would issue from the presses of the Pope.   Less
incense and more newspapers, fewer masses and more
leading articles, and at least one live editor for every
half-dozen cardinals—on those lines much may be
done.

V. *The Social Question.*—On this question there is no
doubt that the Pope means business.   He is, of course,
very far from making common cause with the violent
revolutionaries, whether Anarchists or Collectivists, who
arrogate to themselves the exclusive right to the title of
Socialists.   But he is aiming more or less unconsciously
at establishing the Holy See as the headquarters of a
new International.   He is vigorously pushing on the
organization of industrial circles, a kind of Catholic

trades' union, in France, Spain, and Belgium, and all these circles or labour unions are more or less closely affiliated to Rome. If the programme of the recent Socialist congresses in Paris is compared with the programme of the Pope, there is sufficient resemblance to strike the most casual observer. The Pope is for developing and extending the principle of factory legislation, so as to secure for childhood exemption from labour and liberty to learn. The Pope is for securing for the workman one rest day in seven. The Pope is for shortening the hours of labour. I was very curious to know whether the Pope meant to do anything more than emit counsels of perfection on these subjects. I think if encouraged he will not stop there. He sent Cardinal Lavigerie round Europe to revive the new crusade against the slave trade in Africa. It is quite on the cards that he may send another Cardinal round the world, preaching a still more popular crusade against hours of labour which leave the workman no time to live. Take the question of the six days' working week. They told me that on this subject the Pope is extremely eager. I asked whether his eagerness would carry him far enough to summon an International Conference on the subject. I was assured that there was no conference which the Pope would be more delighted to summon, and if he were well enough, he would gladly preside over such an assembly, to which he would eagerly invite representatives of all Protestant sects and atheistic and revolutionary societies, so long as they would agree to co-operate

in obtaining the great boon of one day's rest in seven.
When that conference meets, I hope I may be there.
Even the Moderator of the Free Kirk would admit that
when he was doing such work, the stoutest Presbyterian
might well follow the lead of the Pope of Rome. The
Pope cannot send delegates to congresses representing
governments. Difficulties would arise with Italy. But
he will watch the proceedings of the Congress at Berne,
and if he sees a chance of striking in to realise the programme which is here arrived at, he will not let the
opportunity slip. We may also expect him to encourage
his clergy everywhere to favour the adoption of Courts of
Conciliation and of Arbitration, as a means of settling
trade disputes. Upon the wider question of capital,
land ownership, and the other issues which go down
deep, I can only add that the Pope's devotion to Thomas
Aquinas may well encourage the more advanced school
to regard the Holy Father as in a hopeful condition.
That, however, is not practical for the moment; and it is
of more importance to know that if the Holy See can
give effect to the volition of its chief, all the mighty army
of Catholic priests will emulate each in his own sphere
the good work of Cardinal Manning and Archbishop
Walsh.

VI. *International Arbitration.*—There is a growing
feeling on the part of the Catholics that the Pope
ought to be Chief Justice of Christendom. Nothing
was more touching than the prayer of the French
peasants and labourers to the Chief Pastor to interpose

to free the toiler from the crushing burden of the armed peace. In Spain, also, of late there has been the manifestation of a similar desire, and in this respect the laity but reflect the aspiration of their spiritual chief. Ever since he succeeded in composing the disputes between Germany and Spain about the Caroline Islands, he has been haunted by a pious ambition to compose all other national disputes in the same fashion. Now that Mr. Henry Richard is dead, nothing would surprise me less than to see his place taken by some eloquent friar. Here also, if the Pope could have his way, the Catholic vote would be cast solid in favour of international arbitration. This may not be the way of peace ; but it indicates an anxiety to seek peace and ensure it, which I note with gratitude.

VII. *The Emancipation of Woman.*—It was on this point that I had most misgivings, and on this point that I left Rome most reassured. The Pope has certainly not yet declared for woman's suffrage. But many of his best advisers find the demand just and logical. And this on two grounds. First, the obvious fact that woman in Europe is the sole hope of the Church. To enfranchise woman would place the Freethinker everywhere in a minority. Secondly, apart from this self-interested view, the Holy See is logically driven to demand the enfranchisement of woman. The Catholic Church has always protested against the intrusion of the State in the question of education. The responsibility rested with the parents, with the mother equally with the father. So

it was in other matters, such as child labour, the nursing
of the sick, sanitation, poor relief, etc., etc.   In all these
matters the State has encroached upon the family.   The
rights usurped by the State were originally exercised by
the husband and the wife.   They were now solely in the
hands of the State, which is monopolised by the male.
Hence as a *pis aller*, to restore to the woman her
original share in the management of the home and the
governance of her children is an obvious duty, upon
which I venture to hope the Church will not fail to
insist.   For morality and religion, the woman's vote is
all-important.   The Pope, in his address to the French
pilgrims, spoke of the *faiblesse et la mission toute
domestique* of woman, a phrase which may be inter-
preted as going counter to the aspirations of woman for
a free career.   The Pope, however, has to speak for all
Christendom; and in great parts of Christendom, to
insist upon the *mission toute domestique* of woman is to
point to an ideal which few have realised.   The degrada-
tion of woman to a beast of burden, who does all the
heavy work while man hunts, or smokes, or goes on
the war-trail, is not yet entirely worked out in many
parts of Europe.   At the same time, the reaction
against this brutality may easily go too far; and
there is always the danger lest, in legislating against
the honest labour of women, you drive them to
means of livelihood infinitely more revolting and
degrading.

In concluding this brief and cursory survey of one of

the widest and most interesting of human problems, I
must say that I end my task in a more hopeful spirit
than when I began. I have not felt in the least the
fascination of Rome. Never was I less inclined to
join the Papal Church than when I stood beneath the
dome of St. Peter's. The great organization at the
centre of which I stood filled me with no sense of its
supernatural wisdom or of its superhuman weight. On
the contrary, the chief conviction which was borne in
upon my mind, on looking at the Papacy more closely,
was a sorrowful sense of the lamentable chasm which
had yawned between the Church and the vital realities
of modern life. It is time the Church came down to
earth again, and saw that even in order to save souls from
hell it is well to take more pains about getting the will of
God done now and here on earth as it is in heaven. There
is nothing like a vivifying contact with solid facts and the
immutable laws which govern our visible life to indoc-
trinate the Church with the scientific spirit, to enable
it to slough its abuses and to bring its quaint ana-
chronisms up to the time of day. There are many
things I do not like about the Church. There are many
of the dogmas that seem to be utterly incredible; its
exaggeration of the virtues of celibacy is simply
lamentable; and if it were strong enough it would probably deem it necessary to burn me at the stake as it
burned Giordano Bruno. But it is necessary to be
charitable even to those who would roast you, and
tolerant of those who are intolerant of you. And no

amount of prejudice can prevent my seeing that there
is great good in the Church, and that there are possibilities in it of much greater good than any which it
has yet realised. The problem is how best to develop
the good and eliminate the bad. Surely the solution is
not difficult. How can you drive out the darkness
better than by letting in the light? How can you keep
the unfruitful works of empty ceremonial and idle
services from encroaching upon the time and the minds
of the faithful than by cultivating the fruitful works of
philanthropy?

When I left Rome night had fallen over the Cam-
pagna, but the summer lightning was playing in splendour over the summits of the Alban Hills. It was
brilliantly beautiful. The whole western sky was lit up
with the lambent flame, which leaped from peak to peak
of the silent hills, as if the ghosts of the old volcanoes
were revisiting the craters from whence the fiery lava
had long ages since rolled hissing toward the sea. But
no thunder followed the lightning; it was but a splendid
display of celestial pyrotechny, which enabled me to gain
another glimpse of the wooded hill behind whose pre-
cipitous slope slept the cool and limpid waters of the
Alban Lake. It seemed no inapt vision writ in fiery
characters across the darkening sky of the present condition of the Catholic Church. Her anathemas are but
as summer lightning, compared with those dread bolts
which hissed and flamed from the Pontiffs who climbed
on Peter's chair to wield Jove's thunder. But although

the volcano has long been extinct, deep in the heart of the mighty crater there lies, like the waters of the Alban Lake, a great store of Christian love and human sympathy, which may yet be made available for quenching the thirst of the world. The old aqueducts are almost as badly broken as those which once brought water to Rome; but the water is there, and the aqueducts may be repaired. Is it not worth while to try?

END.

INDEX.

CASSELL & COMPANY, LIMITED, BELLE SAUVAGE WORKS, LONDON, E.C.